Liguori Sacramental Preparation Series

Your Marriage

PARTICIPANT WORKBOOK

Edited by Deborah Meister

Liguori

Imprimi Potest: Stephen T. Rehrauer, CSsR, Provincial, Denver Province, the Redemptorists

Imprimatur: "In accordance with CIC 827, permission to publish has been granted on April 20, 2015, by the Most Reverend Edward M. Rice, Auxiliary Bishop, Archdiocese of St. Louis. Permission to publish is an indication that nothing contrary to Church teaching is contained in this work. It does not imply any endorsement of the opinions expressed in the publication; nor is any liability assumed by this permission."

Your Marriage Participant Workbook published by Liguori Publications, Liguori, Missouri 63057.
To order, visit Liguori.org or call 800-325-9521.

Copyright © 2015 Liguori Publications

p ISBN 978-0-7648-2546-0
e ISBN 978-0-7648-6999-0

Excerpts from *Vatican Council II: The Basic Sixteen Documents,* Revised Translation, copyright 1996 by Reverend Austin Flannery, OP; published by Costello Publishing Company, Inc., Northport, NY, are used by permission of the publisher. All Rights Reserved.

Excerpts from other Vatican documents are used with permission. Copyright *Libreria Editrice Vaticana* (© *Libreria Editrice Vaticana)*

Excerpts from English translation of the *Catechism of the Catholic Church* for the United States of America © 1994, United States Catholic Conference, Inc.—*Libreria Editrice Vaticana;* English translation of the *Catechism of the Catholic Church: Modifications from the Editio Typica* © 1997, United States Catholic Conference, Inc.—*Libreria Editrice Vaticana.*

Excerpts from the English translation of *Order of Celebrating Matrimony* © 1969, International Commission on English in the Liturgy Corporation. All Rights Reserved.

Scripture texts in this work are taken from the *New American Bible,* revised edition © 2010, 1991, 1986, 1970 Confraternity of Christian Doctrine, Washington, D.C., and are used by permission of the copyright owner. All Rights Reserved. No part of the *New American Bible* may be reproduced in any form without permission in writing from the copyright owner.

Cover design: John Krus   Cover image: Getty Images

Unless noted otherwise, interior images are from Shutterstock.

Liguori Publications, a nonprofit corporation, is an apostolate of the Redemptorists. To learn more about the Redemptorists, visit Redemptorists.com.

Printed in the United States of America
21 20 19 18 17 / 6 5 4 3 2

Acknowledgments

Your Marriage would not have been possible without the diligent service of our publication and production teams.

To the authors, contributors, and editors: Your charity, ministries, personal witnesses, and vocations speak volumes that could not be contained in this program. We and the many parishes and couples who use this program are ever grateful for your wisdom.

To the sacramental-preparation team at Liguori Publications—Wendy Barnes, Angela Baumann, Mark Bernard, Julia DiSalvo, Chuck Healy, Gabriel Hernández, Lorena Jimenez, John Krus, Luis Medina, Bill Townsend, and many other leaders, staff, and customers: Your hard work and feedback shed light on a great need in the Church and shaped a solution for a diverse community.

To the Salt River Production Group, especially Chuck Neff, and our video cast, crew, and team, especially Fr. Byron Miller, CSsR: Thank you for the special and sacred presence you bring to Catholic couples everywhere.

Contents

Congratulations on your engagement!

This workbook contains a wealth of information to help you prepare for the sacrament of matrimony. The Church wants to help you to **be ready not just for your wedding day but for a lifetime together** in marriage, and therefore it asks you to invest time and take this work seriously. Your willingness to participate in this program shows the deep commitment you have to loving one another and to your marriage vows.

The *Code of Canon Law* requires "personal preparation to enter marriage, which disposes the spouses to the holiness and duties of their new state" (*Canon* 1063.2). This time of education and formation, as with all sacramental preparation, is done under the direction of the Church. Most parishes and dioceses require some formal program, and the priest, deacon, coordinator, and/or sponsor couple(s) assisting you in this process will give you further direction on how to use this workbook.

You may be asked to attend a series of meetings or a retreat that will guide you through this workbook and help you to discuss the questions at the end of each chapter. Whether or not you answer every one or touch on every subject in the sessions, we recommend you **read all the material and complete the exercises** as a couple before the wedding. The final four chapters do not apply to every couple. These will be assigned according to need at your leader's discretion. In the end, the responsibility of preparing for marriage rests with the two of you. May God continue to bless you today and all the days of your life.

Deborah Meister, editor

Opening Prayer

Loving God, you have called us here this day
  to prepare as best we can for the Sacrament of Matrimony.

Bless us with the grace we need to open our hearts and minds
  to the holy mystery of marriage.

We desire to live as man and wife with a love that never fails.

Bless our conversations and our quiet moments with your wisdom.

We rely on the foundation of faith and prayer in building a strong marriage.

Bless our love with the grace to be forgiving and unselfish.

We desire to let our marriage shine with the love and light of Christ
  to be a sign of your unconditional and everlasting love for the whole world.

Amen.

Closing Prayer

O God, your love and compassion speak to us through one another.

You have called us here (today/tonight) to reflect on and understand better
  the lifelong covenant with one another in marriage.

Help us to be open to the grace we need to prepare well,
  to truly discern our vows, and to prepare ourselves to build a strong marriage.

Thank you for your presence as we continue to share all that we have received
  and grow in love and unity.

Bless our conversations and help us to see your face in one another.

Amen.

Spirituality and Faith in Marriage

Deacon Harold Burke-Sivers

In this chapter...

- Christ is the foundation of the domestic church.
- Faith within marriage can be challenging.
- How to share a life of prayer

When a man and a woman marry, they make a permanent decision to love—to make a complete gift of self to the other in love that is free, faithful, total, and fruitful. On their wedding day, through the grace of the sacrament, they enter into a profoundly intimate and life-giving relationship in communion with the Lord. With Christ's help, they establish a strong foundation upon which to build their married life.

This foundation, this support structure, is the covenant love of Jesus Christ. Just as Jesus held nothing back, broke himself open, and poured himself out for us—husbands and wives are called by God and gifted by his Spirit to love, service, and sacrifice. When they open their hearts and take up this mission, they make themselves vulnerable and create a gift not just to God and each other, but to the rest of the world.

Make Jesus the cornerstone of your marriage.

PSALM 127

"Unless the LORD build the house, they labor in vain who build."

Name three things your relationship is based on.

1. _____
2. _____
3. _____

MATTHEW 7:24

"Everyone who listens to these words of mine and acts on them will be like a wise man who built his house on rock."

Name three things you hope to build in your life together.

1. _____
2. _____
3. _____

JOHN 13:15

"I have given you a model to follow, so that as I have done for you, you should also do."

Name three ways you already model Christ's love, service, or sacrifice.

1. _____
2. _____
3. _____

JOHN 4:12

"If we love one another, God remains in us, and his love is brought to perfection in us."

Name three ways you hope to improve your love as you enter marriage.

1. _____
2. _____
3. _____

Challenges for Spiritual Marriages

Attitudes and expressions of faith shape a couple's marriage and shared spiritual life. When practices and preferences are not understood or valued, tension and stress can result. If you are preparing for an interchurch or interfaith marriage, another chapter in this workbook is just for you.

Consider:
- Mass attendance (weekly, daily)
- Devotions
- Religious objects, especially in the home
- Bible study
- Religious events and presentations
- Charity and service
- Evangelization
- Faith-based political activity

Different Religious Practices

In the table below, list specific practices that fit each category for you, then share and compare with your partner. We'll deal with prayer preferences next.

Current and Valued	Familiar or Desired	Neutral or Unsure	Disliked or Avoided	Objectionable

Faith Gap

Often one spouse will grow in his or her faith while the other doesn't, or they will grow in different ways. While respecting each other's gifts and spiritual journeys, never presuming that the other will change simply to please us, every effort should be made to maintain a strong faith connection through prayer, patience, and humility. By seeking to grow in faith and holiness together, the Lord assures us that the truth will set us free (John 8:32).

Praying Together

Many couples have not prayed together in a long time, if ever. Just as couples must talk to get to know each other and show affection to feel closer, it is not possible to get to know God or grow closer to Christ as a couple without approaching him together.

Prayer is both a gift of grace and a response to God's invitation to a covenant relationship. Prayer enables husbands and wives to listen to God's voice, walk humbly in the obedience of faith, and recommit themselves to love and intimacy with him and each other. Spouses need God's help every step of the way, both in good times and bad. When spouses pray out of anxiety, they reflect their trust in God and enter into the heart of Christ's passion and death. Jesus promises, "All that you ask for in prayer, believe that you will receive it and it shall be yours" (Mark 11:24). God knows your deepest longings and desires to bring you closer to each other and him.

Many couples believe it's enough to go to church on Sunday, pray before meals, or maintain a personal prayer life. They may not know how to pray together or fear it would be uncomfortable or awkward. How do spouses overcome this, especially if they have different prayer styles? The key is to keep it simple and keep working at it.

Suggestions

Find a mutually agreeable time and place and aim to spend a few minutes together in daily prayer.

Start with a moment of silence, then take turns leading or reciting a simple, traditional prayer.

Have each spouse share a favorite prayer or offer a few personal petitions or intentions. Do not be afraid to say what is in your hearts.

Read a Scripture passage and reflect on what it means to them as a couple.

The Benefits of Praying Together

- Increased affection, respect, and esteem toward each other;
- A deeper commitment to seeking God together;
- Greater honesty, trust, and appreciation between the spouses;
- Developing loving habits that will become part of their everyday life;
- Rekindling the love, joy, and passion of their relationship.

Determining a Common Prayer Style

	Woman	Man
1. When praying, I like to:		
a. Sit	Y	N
b. Stand	Y	N
c. Kneel	Y	N
d. Walk	Y	N
2. I like to use set prayers of the Church (such as Rosary, Liturgy of the Hours, Novenas, Our Father, Hail Mary).	Y	N
3. I enjoy spontaneous prayer from the heart.	Y	N
4. I enjoy praying in silence.	Y	N
5. I enjoy praying out loud.	Y	N
6. I enjoy listening to spiritual music while I pray.	Y	N
7. I enjoy Scripture reading and/or *lectio divina.*	Y	N
8. I enjoy meditative or contemplative prayer.	Y	N
9. I like to pray in the morning.	Y	N
10. I like to pray at night.	Y	N
11. I like to pray in short intervals throughout the day.	Y	N
12. I like praying in our bedroom.	Y	N
13. I like praying outside.	Y	N
14. I like praying in the car.	Y	N
15. I like to create an environment for prayer (such as candle(s), crucifix, holy pictures).	Y	N

- Write down the numbered statements where you both answered "yes."

- Decide how you will incorporate what you both enjoy into a shared experience of prayer. Prayer is intimate, so be clear about your privacy expectations and set clear boundaries.

- After your prayer time, briefly share how you are feeling. Occasionally review how things are going. Ask each other:
    1. What has God said to you during our prayer time?
    2. Are you comfortable? Do you feel less vulnerable and more secure?
    3. Do you look forward to our prayer time?
    4. What can we do to make praying together even better?

Forming Your Faith

Learning is an essential part of spirituality. Just as the body needs nourishment, the soul does not grow when one's faith is not fed. Studying the Bible and learning how to integrate prayer and sacraments into everyday life should be a part of the journey. By forming their faith and consciences according to Christ, the spouses truly encounter him, and the Word will become flesh in their married life.

The Domestic Church

Spirituality in marriage spills over into family life. Families help each member discover their vocation and develop virtues. The Holy Family—Jesus, Mary, and Joseph—model how to carry out the roles of father, mother, and child. The Children and Parenting chapter dives deeper into the importance of Christian parenting, especially regarding:

† Modeling and witnessing to covenantal love

† Establishing faith traditions as a family

† Creating a Christ-centered atmosphere in the home

† Forming and educating children in the faith

† Supporting and tapping into, rather than relying on, the parish, schools, and community.

Individual Prayer

Praying as a couple should never replace the active, fruitful prayer life of each spouse. In marriage, the two become one flesh, but not one person. In marriage, husbands and wives do not lose anything of their individual selves—they actually become more of the person God created and called them to be. Each spouse's relationship with God benefits the whole family by nourishing his or her soul and enhancing the couple's shared prayer life.

The **wedding vows** are a promise to cherish and support each other all the days of your lives. Husbands and wives must allow the fire of God's love to purify their lives and relationship. When spouses live a vibrant, courageous spirituality, the Holy Spirit will consume them, and their love will be transformed. This is not always easy, but spouses should receive confidence from the grace of their sacrament. With God, all things are possible!

For Reflection and Discussion

1. How would you describe your personal relationship with God and prayer life?

2. How has your relationship with God changed since meeting your future spouse?

3. The life of a married couple in today's world is often hectic. Name three ways that you can make a gift of yourself to your spouse.

4. Name two or three ways the two of you have made sacrifices to strengthen your relationship.

5. Take turns completing this phrase: *I see God in you when...*

_____

_____

_____

_____

_____

_____

_____

_____

_____

_____

_____

_____

_____

_____

_____

_____

_____

_____

Theology of Marriage

David W. Fagerberg, PhD

In this chapter...

- What makes marriage unique?
- What are the "goods" of marriage?
- What is meant by "natural law?"

Marriage is often called "the first sacrament," or primordial sacrament, because it existed in the Garden of Eden, even before the Fall. With a father's tenderness, God brought Adam and Eve together and wished them happiness. "God Himself is the author of matrimony, endowed as it is with various benefits and purposes" (*Gaudium et Spes,* 48). Therefore, marriage is not the state's idea for landscaping a society or society's plan for organizing itself. **Marriage comes from the mind of the Creator when he wills the happiness and fulfillment of his creatures.**

The vocation to marriage is written in the very nature of man and woman as they came from the hand of the Creator. Marriage is not a purely human institution despite the many variations it may have undergone through the centuries in different cultures, social structures, and spiritual attitudes. These differences should not cause us to forget its common and permanent characteristics.

CCC *1603*

Questions of marriage hang in the air—put to us by the divorce rate, single parents, anonymous sex, LGBT unions, and so forth. People wonder:

- *Why bother getting married? Isn't it just a piece of paper?*

- *Why try to maintain an imperfect marriage or repair a damaged one?*

- *Why limit its protections and benefits to certain relationships?*

The Church offers three answers, which we call "the goods of marriage":

✚ *bonum prolis*
the good of offspring

✚ *bonum fidei*
the good of chaste fidelity

✚ *bonum sacramenti*
the good of an unbreakable bond

These may sound like difficult theological concepts, but when we study their meanings and founding principles, we can find their deep truth.

The word **bonum**, meaning "**good**," can be understood as a value or blessing. **Something is good when it accomplishes the end for which it is made**: a good pen writes, a good knife cuts, a good watch tells time. Something is good when it possesses the perfections proper to its nature. This leads us to ask, "What is the nature of marriage? What makes it different from every other relationship?" You have friendships, associates and business relationships, and social acquaintances. But these three **goods** distinguish the marital relationship from any other.

What Makes Marriage Special?

Most common items have a right and proper nature. Consider the examples below, then complete the table using another example of your choosing:

Item	Spatula	Automobile	
Proper and Natural Purpose(s)	Scraping, smoothing, flipping	Transporting people and goods	
Other Uses (proper or improper)	Swatting	Ramming, pulling, pushing	
Competing Item(s)	Knife	Train, bike, airplane, boat	
Exclusive or Supreme?	Nonexclusive, but often supreme	Nonexclusive, but superior in some cases	

Marriage is unlike anything else, unique from and above other relationships in three ways:

1. Marriage is only between a man and woman who can be "ministers of omnipotence" and create new life.

2. Marriage is between one man and one woman living in exclusive fidelity to each other.

3. Once sealed, marriage is unbreakable by any human being, including the spouses themselves.

Think about these things in terms of your own experiences. Will a parent, teacher, or business partner fulfill you for life? Can a friendship ever grow closer without becoming more and more committed, exclusive, and intimate? Indeed, many marriages begin as friendships.

The following shows where certain relationships imitate the qualities of marriage and where they fall short.

Name	Sophia	Jackie	Ron
Relationship	Best Friend	Mother	Coworker
Proper and Natural Purpose(s)	Fellowship, encouragement	Care and nurturing, formation	Cooperative labor and service
Reproductive Potential? (Y/N)	Yes	Yes	No
Exclusive or Supreme? (Y/N)	Perhaps, but not always	Exclusive if an only child but not supreme	No
Consensual? (Y/N)	Yes	No (a child is not developmentally capable of true consent, and parents do not specifically select their children)	Yes
Unbreakable? (Y/N)	No	Biologically, yes	No

Select two people, other than your fiancé(e) with whom you have a relationship. Complete the chart for those individuals as was done on page 23.

Name		
Relationship		
Proper and Natural Purpose(s)		
Reproductive Potential? (Y/N)		
Exclusive or Supreme? (Y/N)		
Consensual? (Y/N)		
Unbreakable? (Y/N)		

Now think about your future spouse. Besides the distinguishing factors of marriage, **name a few other ways** in which your relationship is unique. Consider your personalities, shared interests, values, and other factors.

The Goods of Marriage

Bonum prolis
The Good of Children

In his 1930 encyclical on Christian marriage, *Casti Connubii*, Pope Pius XI wrote that marriage is "the means of transmitting life, thus making the parents the ministers, as it were, of the Divine Omnipotence" (80). Incredibly, God shares with mother and father the privilege of bringing life into the world: They become ministers of his power to create. This distinguishes the married covenant between one man and one woman from any other relationship.

Some people perceive a conflict between this procreative good and the unitive good of intercourse—even though there is none. As far back as the fifth century, St. Augustine emphasized that marriage benefited the whole of society and not only the two people begetting children. He reminds us that although offspring is a significant good, it is not the only good, and he disapproves of the ancient Roman practice of men divorcing their wives when they cannot bear any more children. The bond is tied for the sake of begetting children, true, but it cannot be loosed even when the parents are not blessed with children.

The good of children in marriage means more than just having babies, anyway. Christian marriages create families in which

new citizens of human society are born, who by the grace of the Holy Spirit received in baptism are made children of God, thus perpetuating the people of God through the centuries. The family is, so to speak, the domestic church.

Lumen Gentium, *11*

Marriage embeds a child within a nurturing community of father and mother who both see to his or her development, education, and formation. Parenting is creation-in-action, because it brings forth personhood. **Marriage is about love; and love mimics the Trinity.** The persons of the Trinity pour themselves out to each other and to all creation; therefore, married love gives itself not only from spouse to spouse, but also to others. This is why Catholic doctrine asks the couple to be open to life. It is the basis of Catholic teaching on contraception. It is not just about the children, it is about the relationship between the husband and wife. Not being open to life in sexual intercourse alters the total self-giving.

Bonum fidei

The Good of Chaste Fidelity

Chastity is an upright fortitude that integrates sexuality into a person's life. Aristotle said justice is doing the right thing, at the right time, for the right reason, in the right measure, in the right way. Therefore, chastity is sexuality practiced justly. Therefore, "all the baptized are called to chastity" (*CCC* 2348) and should cultivate it in a way suited to his or her state of life. Married people live conjugal chastity; vowed religious practice chastity in continence; and single persons let chastity blossom under charity in friendship (*CCC* 2349, 2346).

Fidelity is no less difficult a word to grasp. We all respect fidelity. No one would allow a groom to promise on his wedding day to "love, honor, and obey until I no longer feel like it." But as a society, we struggle to believe that complete fidelity is possible.
On your wedding day, you don't promise to feel the same way every day—that's impossible. We all go through various moods; there are unforeseen events ahead. **What you *do* promise is to place whatever changes you undergo, all decisions and delights, into the context of this promise.**

Fidelity is required for the mutual growth and perfection of man and woman. Pope Pius XI said, "This mutual molding of husband and wife [can] be said to be the chief reason and purpose of matrimony" (*Casti Connubii*, 24). But this effort is not directed toward your ideal image of a husband or wife, but rather to God's spiritual design. Your spouse is a tool in the hands of the Holy Spirit, which is why your choice of a spouse is a spiritual decision as well as a personal one.

---

chas·ti·ty

A spiritual energy capable of defending love from the perils of selfishness and aggressiveness, and able to advance it towards its full realization

Familiaris Consortio, 33

Theology in Action

ISAIAH 54:5

"Your husband is your Maker; the LORD of hosts is his name, Your redeemer, the Holy One of Israel, called God of all the earth."

Name three ways God has shown his love and fidelity to you.

1. _____
2. _____
3. _____

REVELATION 19:7

"The wedding day of the Lamb has come, his bride has made herself ready."

Name three tasks/goals you have for your marriage preparation.

1. _____
2. _____
3. _____

EPHESIANS 5:25

"Husbands, love your wives, even as Christ loved the church…"

Name three ways you see God present and active within the Christian community and/or your local church.

1. _____
2. _____
3. _____

JOHN 3:29

"The one who has the bride is the bridegroom; the best man, who stands and listens to him, rejoices greatly…"

Name three ways you can (or do) support the institution of marriage.

1. _____
2. _____
3. _____

Bonum sacramenti

The Good of an Unbreakable Bond

Christ elevates natural marriage to sacramental marriage when it is between two baptized Christians (not just Catholics). The *Catechism* states, "in a Christian marriage the spouses are strengthened and, as it were, consecrated for the duties and the dignity of their state by a special sacrament." A sacramental marriage is a liturgical act, which is why the Church normally requires marriage according to the established Christian form.

Catholic teaching is adamant that a marriage only comes about by the free choice of two persons. **However, once consent is freely given, a reality comes into existence that no longer depends on the person's will or intentions.**

The sacramental bond of marriage cannot be undone, because the covenant, "established by God," has created a fact, an actuality, that doesn't exist just in feelings or the imagination (or on paper), but in reality. In the Bible, a covenant is equal in binding force to a blood relationship. It lasts until death. And that is the very point. The two have become one.

From a valid marriage arises a bond between the spouses which by its very nature is perpetual and exclusive....

(*CCC* 1638)

Unlike a contract, the marriage doesn't collapse when one party violates the terms or withdraws consent. The promise itself, **the grace of the sacrament, will carry the spouses through times of lessened resolve.** This power, like God's fidelity toward all, is something to celebrate and in which to have faith.

Church teachings about marriage come from the teachings of Jesus. Although the law of Moses allowed divorce, Christ says he has come to restore the original order of creation disturbed by sin.

Jesus raised marriage under the natural law to function within the supernatural law. **This indissoluble bond is the hidden thing—the *sacramentum*, the mystery—that makes marriage a deeper sign of something else.**

This bond, which results from the free human act of the spouses and their consummation of the marriage, is a reality, henceforth irrevocable, and gives rise to a covenant guaranteed by God's fidelity. The Church does not have the power to contravene this disposition of divine wisdom (CCC 1640).

A Timeless Sacrament

When the church speaks of "the sacrament of marriage," it is not only speaking about the wedding. Although the ceremony and rite are wonderful, the whole marriage, the relationship itself, is the sacrament. A marriage of fifty or sixty years is a well-aged sacrament that merely began with a one-hour ceremony.

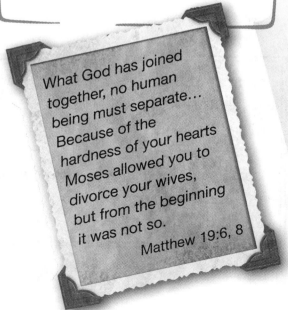

What God has joined together, no human being must separate... Because of the hardness of your hearts Moses allowed you to divorce your wives, but from the beginning it was not so.

Matthew 19:6, 8

Rising Above

The three goods of marriage are directed to our happiness. They exist in an ascending relationship to each other, building upon each other. With his systematic mind St. Thomas Aquinas noticed this.

Marriage is a...	for the good of...	to perpetuate...	and is governed by...
Natural institution	Nature	the Human race	Natural law
Social institution	Society	the Family and State	Civil law
Sacrament	the Church	Christian faith	Divine law

This is not hard to understand; we use the language of "higher and lower" all the time. Take, for example, food:

"Good" of Food	Example	Purpose(s)
Biological (high)	Daily meals	Sustenance
Human / Social (higher)	Catered banquet	Pleasure, hospitality, romance
Spiritual (highest)	Eucharist	Union with Christ and Church, sanctifying grace

Complete the ascending goods for the following attributes.

As you enter your marriage, aim high!

Washing	Example	Purpose(s)
Biological		
Human / Social		
Spiritual		

Art	Example	Purpose(s)
Biological		
Human / Social		
Spiritual		

What Is Natural Law?

Natural law is often misunderstood because of the way people use the word "natural." Frequently, it is used to mean anything free from human influence (a bear lives by natural law in the woods, or natural ingredients have not been processed). But it **means more than just "whatever we happen to find"** or **"whatever we instinctually feel."** People do all sorts of things "naturally," not all of them good.

Natural law is the reflection of Divine Wisdom (God) in human nature. When God's providence directs the sun in its orbit it is called a law of nature; when it directs a rational creature it is called natural law.

> *The rational creature...has a share*
> *of the Eternal Reason,*
> *whereby it has a natural inclination*
> *to its proper act and end:*
> *and this participation of the eternal*
> *law in the rational creature is*
> *called the natural law.*
>
> —St. Thomas Aquinas

Animals are directed by instinct, but rational men and women have something over and above instinct; they receive laws spoken to their reason.

The *Catechism* states that natural law is engraved in the soul of every person, and by its moral sense they "discerned by reason the good and the evil, the truth and the lie" (*CCC* 1954).

Natural law is immutable and permanent, which is why it applies to all persons at all times. The Church's teaching about marriage is rooted in nature itself as designed by God. Scripture tells us, "it is not good for man to be alone" (Genesis 2:18). **According to natural law, marriage is one and indissoluble**. Natural law guides civil law to respect the common good, including marriage, and civil law cannot change it. Marriage exists because human nature comes in two complementary sexes, male and female, and their union is a marital act.

Marriage is rooted in nature itself as designed by God...Natural law guides civil law, and civil law cannot change it.

A Fourth Good?

All three goods of marriage—children, fidelity, and indissoluble unity—are meant to serve the good of the spouses, which might be called a **bonum conjugum**. Although this was not one of the original three, we understand the good of the spouses to be in the three goods taken together. The *Code of Canon Law* affirms it by describing marriage as being ordered toward "the good of the spouses and the procreation and education of offspring" (*Canon* 1055). The *Catechism* says this:

> The marriage covenant, by which a man and a woman form with each other an intimate communion of life and love, has been founded and endowed with its own special laws by the Creator. By its very nature it is ordered to the good of the couple, as well as to the generation and education of children.
>
> CCC 1660

For Reflection and Discussion

1. What makes the marriage relationship unique? Discuss how you feel about being a minister of the Divine Omnipotence.

2. Discuss with one another the connection between marriage and parenting. Why do they come together?

3. What have you heard—either through friends, family, or the media—about "chastity?" How does it compare to the definition in this chapter? How would you describe "conjugal chastity?"

4. If the unbreakable bond is a blessing, a good, a value, why do you think some people resist it? Share examples of how your relationship reflects the unity and permanence to come.

5. Share with your future spouse how you hope your marriage will make you a better person and a better Christian.

My Thoughts

Order of Celebrating Matrimony

David W. Fagerberg, PhD

In this chapter...

- Marriage is effected through the exchange of consent.
- As a sacrament, the Order of Celebrating Matrimony is often celebrated within the Mass.
- Within the rite, there are opportunities to personalize the ceremony.

Your Marriage

The word *conjugal* means "to join together," and in the Order of Celebrating Matrimony, that is what the bride and groom do; that is what the community witnesses; that is what the Church receives and blesses and strengthens.

The irrevocable consent is the deed to be done: It "makes the marriage" (*Canon 1057*). **Without free consent, there is no marriage** because it is the required internal state. That internal state is expressed by vows and promises and signified by various cultural expressions, most commonly by exchanging rings. But consent is the essence of the act. The partners freely give themselves to each other and accept each other. According to the Latin tradition (Western Christianity), **the bride and groom minister the sacrament to each other**: "The spouses as ministers of Christ's grace mutually confer upon each other the Sacrament of Matrimony by expressing their consent before the Church" (*CCC 1623*).

The liturgical celebration should manifest the fact that the husband and wife are now undertaking a special vocation in the Christian community. The love they received as a gift from God becomes a gift to the whole Church and to the world. This is not "the bride's day" (or anyone else's); it is a liturgical day. Like all sacramental rites, the marriage liturgy is an act of worship and grace. **The entire liturgy should reflect the fact that they consider their love to be sacred, meaning it belongs to God.** Something already sacred to God is being lifted up to be a sacrament of the new creation. Bride and groom are unified with Christ's love on the cross, which streams forth from his resurrection.

The Basic Structure

Sometimes the Order of Celebrating Matrimony will take place without Mass, perhaps out of necessity, or in the case of a Catholic marrying someone who is not Catholic. **The wedding is still a sacrament, even if there is no Mass, so long as both partners are baptized Christians.** Here we will examine a marriage within Mass.

A wedding takes place in a church for a more profound reason than the couple wanting to be in a beautiful building. Marriage is one of the seven sacraments, a manifestation of God's presence and self-giving love, so it is naturally drawn toward the source and summit of love and self-gift: Christ's paschal mystery celebrated in holy communion. When spouses marry it is fitting they seal their consent by...

uniting it to the offering of Christ for his Church made present in the Eucharistic sacrifice, and by receiving the Eucharist so that...they may form but "one body" in Christ.

CCC *1621*

Every Mass consists of two halves: the Liturgy of the Word, and the Liturgy of the Eucharist. When the Church celebrates a special rite within Mass (a "ritual Mass"), it places the act in the middle. So the joining of the couple is enclosed between and supported by these two parts. The Mass will appear quite familiar, but with adaptations.

Structure of the Wedding Ceremony

1. Introductory rites
2. Liturgy of the Word
3. *Celebration of marriage*
   (a) Questions before consent
   (b) The consent (vows)
   (c) Reception of consent
   (d) Blessing and giving of rings
4. Liturgy of the Eucharist
   (a) Nuptial blessing
5. Conclusion of the celebration

Introductory Rites

Two forms are provided for bringing everyone to the altar.

1. The bridal party is welcomed by the priest and servers at the doors of the church. Then during the entrance chant the procession goes forward in the order of servers, ministers, presider, and the couple, who may be escorted by their parents and/or the two witnesses (usually the best man and maid/matron of honor).

2. The priest waits for the bridal party at his chair or the place prepared for the couple. When the bride and groom have arrived at their place, he welcomes them.

In ancient cultures, marriages were treated as an economic or political contract between families, which gave rise to the tradition of the father "giving away the bride" to a waiting groom. But since Catholic doctrine believes the bride and groom are equal partners giving themselves to each other, the Order of Celebrating Matrimony encourages them to walk in together. As the ministers of this sacrament, it is appropriate that they proceed last.

In both forms, the priest welcomes them and invites the families and friends to support them with affection, friendship, and prayer. He asks the Lord to send help from heaven and protect them. There is no penitential rite at a marriage, but the **Gloria** is sung.

Weddings and the Church Year

While couples may have logistical, sentimental, or other considerations when selecting their wedding date, the Church discourages having weddings during Lent, Advent, and other days of penitence. The somber nature of these feasts neither reflects nor is conducive to the joyous nature of matrimony. If you have a legitimate reason for not avoiding these times, explain your situation and preferences to your pastor or presider. In any case, weddings are celebrated in white or gold vestments to symbolize joy, light, and purity.

The Collect

The opening prayer, called the Collect, is adapted for the wedding. Six options may be considered, and they speak of such things as:

- the bond of inseperable love
- the wedding covenant foreshadowing the sacrament of Christ and his Church
- confirming the love between husband and wife
- the enrichment of the Church with faithful offspring, and
- the binding of marriage in mutual affection, likeness of mind, and shared holiness.

Liturgy of the Word

Scripture proclaims God's covenantal fidelity throughout history. There are abundant passages to choose from, and it is customary for the bride and groom to select them. Each reading reflects biblical teaching about marriage, its foundation, and its blessings.

The Gospel is followed by a homily, which should speak of the mystery of Christian marriage, the grace of the sacrament, and the responsibilities of spouses. Every homily should apply the Scripture to a particular point in our life, and here its focus is on the dignity of conjugal love.

Reflect on a Wedding Reading.

Select one reading option from the Order of Celebrating Matrimony and read it together. Complete the following sentences, then share and discuss your responses
with your partner. See pages 52 and 53.

 The word or phrase that catches me is...

 The character I relate to most is...

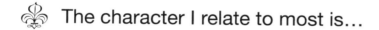 I would summarize the message as...

 I am living out this reading by...

Celebration of Marriage

Now occurs the first insertion—the Celebration of Marriage. It unfolds over four steps, each concern the giving of consent. If two or more couples are celebrating their marriages within the same ceremony, steps 2-4 must take place individually for each couple.

1. **An invitation to state their intent**. The priest reminds the couple they have come to commit themselves to marriage and have it blessed and strengthened with a sacred seal, so they may be faithful to each other and to the responsibilities of married life.

2. Each couple is asked **three questions about their intent and responds separately**:
   a. *Do they enter marriage without coercion, freely, and wholeheartedly?*
   b. *Will they love and honor each other?*
   c. *Will they accept children lovingly from God?*

3. **The consent, or statement of vows.** "Because consent is what makes the marriage, the vows must be clear. There are two forms by which the couple can state their intent ("I, N., take you, N., to be my...”). But it is preferable for the priest to obtain consent through questioning ("N., do you take N., to be your wife... your husband?")

4. **Reception of consent:** The priest asks God to strengthen the consent they have declared, and bring it to fulfillment.

   To what do spouses consent, promise, and agree? To the love and fidelity each is giving to the other, to forfeiting exclusive rights to themselves, to be a sacramental sign of God's love, and to the new role they are assuming in the Church and in the world.

Blessing and Giving of Rings

The rings are a symbolic sign of the new bond, the love and fidelity that has come into being. There are three blessings to choose from. All ask for God's blessings on the rings—that they be a sign of love and fidelity, that those who wear them remain faithful to each other, or that the rings remind them of their love for each other. Husband and wife each place a ring on the other's finger, asking it to be received as a sign of love and fidelity.

Universal Prayer

Since marriage touches many people—families, friends, communities—it is good for the **Universal Prayer** (or commonly "petitions") from the wedding to deliberately radiate outward. The bride and groom are encouraged to choose from examples or to write their own intercessions with guidance from their presider. Of course, prayer for the newly married is appropriate, but the intercessions also embrace all married persons, relatives, friends, and families throughout the world, the poor and homeless, the protection and sanctity of human life, and unity among Christians.

Pray for Us.

One common way to develop petitions is to reflect on your various social and spiritual circles and their respective and apparent needs—moving from closest to furthest, and addressing the **personal, extended,** and **universal** aspects of each area:

Area	Personal	Extended	Universal
Church	Parishes, clergy, and spiritual practices	Dioceses, bishops, sacraments, and teachings	Global church(es), poor, needy, and oppressed
Civic / Social	Coworkers, classmates, neighbors, social clubs	Corporate or government leaders, local or state needs	National and international agencies, industry leaders
Marriage	Bride and groom	Married friends and family	Husbands, wives, Christian spouses
Family	Parents, siblings, children	Grandparents, cousins, stepfamilies	Deceased or distant relatives, the domestic church, human race

With your fiancé(e), select one group, subject, or cause you wish to pray for and fill in each space with specific names, titles, or needs.

Area	Personal	Extended	Universal

Put your prayer into words, turning it into a petition.

Petition: _____

_____

_____

_____

...We pray to the Lord.

Lord, hear our prayer.

Liturgy of the Eucharist

There are four Eucharistic Prayers, and each has a fixed portion and a variable preface. The variable portions focus upon the dignity of the marriage covenant as an abiding sign of God's love and remind us that God created us—and marriage—out of charity, to which we are now called.

After the **Eucharistic Prayer** and the **Our Father**, but before Communion, the second insertion in the Mass occurs. This is the **Nuptial Blessing**, for which the bride and groom either approach the altar or kneel at their place. The priest invites those present to pray that the Lord would pour out his grace on the bride and groom and the Holy Spirit be sent down. It implores God to enable the bride and groom to keep the commandments, be blameless in all they do, bear true witness to Christ, and be blessed with children.

The **Sign of Peace** is given, and **Communion**, if celebrated, is received. The **prayer after Communion** invokes God's aid for the new couple, and the **final blessing**, also adapted toward the couple, concludes the Mass. The options here pray that God keep them in one heart, find the peace of Christ abiding in their homes, and make them witnesses to charity and a comfort to all who come to them in need.

The **recession** is a simple walk out of the church, beginning with the new husband and wife.

Going Forth

God the Father established natural marriage as a union of a man and woman in one flesh. God the Son raised this institution to the dignity of a sacrament, making it a sign of his union with the Church. And God the Spirit walks with the couple on their way toward heaven. After all, marriage gives life to others, and through it, surrounded by the Church's care and protection, spouses find their full human realization.

Wedding Ceremony Planner

This planner will help you determine and organize your wedding details. While it assumes a celebration within a Mass, it can be adapted to your circumstances. Full listings and other resources can be obtained from your presider or parish.

Date, Time, Location

Wedding Day _____

Mass/Ceremony Time _____

Parish/Chapel _____

Address _____

Reception Time(s) _____

Reception Location _____

Address _____

Meal Served At _____

The Wedding Party

Often, the wedding party comprises close relatives and friends with places of honor and may include children to carry the rings, flowers, and other special items. Besides the bride, groom, presider, and two witnesses, these roles are not liturgically necessary.

Groom _____   Bride _____

Groom's Parent(s)   Bride's Parent(s)

_____   _____

_____   _____

Presider _____

Witness / Best Man _____

Witness / Maid of Honor _____

Wedding Party, *continued*

_____   _____

_____   _____

_____   _____

_____   _____

Wedding Ministers

These people serve liturgical functions and may be selected, appointed, or perhaps consolidated to the presider and/or wedding party. Your wedding location and the size of your guest list determine your needs, so speak with your presider or parish about your options.

Usher(s) / Greeter(s) (also consider guest book attendance and program or favor distribution)

_____

_____

Altar Server(s)

_____

_____

Cantor / Musician(s) (in a Mass setting, trained liturgical musicians are recommended over secular performers and recordings)

_____

_____

Lector(s) (one to three are needed for the First Reading, Second Reading, and Universal Prayer)

_____

_____

Eucharistic Minister(s) (also consider a couple or family to bring up the Offertory gifts)

_____

_____

The Rite

Entrance Rite / Procession

Choose one option:

1. Presider meets bride and groom at the door(s) of the church

2. Presider meets bride and groom at the altar
   (The presider is not in the procession.)

3. Bride and groom process together, followed by:
   - ∞ Servers and ministers
   - ∞ Presider
   - ∞ Wedding party
   - ∞ Witnesses and/or parents
   - ∞ Bride and groom

4. Bride and groom process escorted (normal order follows):
   - ∞ Servers and ministers
   - ∞ Presider
   - ∞ Wedding party
   - ∞ Groom, escorted by [parent(s) / witness]
   - ∞ Bride, escorted by [parent(s) / witness]

Liturgy of the Word

Choose at least one reading that explicitly speaks of marriage, as indicated by the asterisk.

First Reading, Old Testament

⚭ Genesis 1:26–28, 31*: "God created man in his image; …male and female he created them."

⚭ Genesis 2:18–24*: "It is not good for the man to be alone….That is why…the two of them become one body."

⚭ Genesis 24:48–51, 58–67*: "Isaac took Rebekah into his tent; he married her, and thus she became his wife."

⚭ Tobit 7:6-14*: "Your marriage to her has been decided in heaven! …from now on you are her love, and she is your beloved."

⚭ Tobit 8:4b-8*: "Lord, you know that I take this wife of mine not because of lust, but for a noble purpose. Call down your mercy…and allow us to live together to a happy old age."

⚭ Proverbs 31:10–13, 19–20, 30–31*: "When one finds a worthy wife, her value is far beyond pearls."

⚭ Song of Songs 2:8–10, 14, 16; 8:6–7: "Set me as a seal on your heart…."

⚭ Sirach 26:1–4, 13–16*: "Blessed the husband of a good wife…."

⚭ Jeremiah 31:31–34: "I will place my law within them, and write it upon their hearts."

Responsorial Psalm

These hymns of ancient Israel are full of nuptial imagery.

⚭ Psalm 33
⚭ Psalm 34
⚭ Psalm 103
⚭ Psalm 112
⚭ Psalm 128*
⚭ Psalm 145
⚭ Psalm 148

Second Reading, New Testament

⚭ Romans 8:31–35, 37–39: "What will separate us from the love of Christ?"

⚭ Romans 12:1–2, 9–18: "Offer your bodies as a living sacrifice, holy and pleasing to God, your spiritual worship…Let love be sincere…."

⚭ Romans 15:1–3, 5–7, 13: "May the God of endurance and encouragement grant you to think in harmony with one another."

⚭ 1 Corinthians 6:13–15, 17–20: "Do you not know that your body is a temple of the Holy Spirit…?"

⚭ 1 Corinthians 12:31 – 13:8: "Love is patient, love is kind."

⚭ Ephesians 4:1-6 : I…urge you to live in a manner worthy of the call you have received…"

⚭ Ephesians 5:2, 21–33*: "Husbands, love your wives, even as Christ loved the Church…."

⚭ Philippians 4:4–9: "Rejoice in the Lord always… if there is anything worthy of praise, think about these things."

⚭ Colossians 3:12–17: "Over all these put on love, that is, the bond of perfection."

⚭ Hebrews 13:1–6*: "Let mutual love continue… Let marriage be honored among all…."

⚭ 1 Peter 3:1–9*: "All of you, be of one mind, sympathetic, loving toward one another…."

⚭ 1 John 3:18–24: "His commandment is this: we should believe in the name of his Son, Jesus Christ, and love one another…."

⚭ 1 John 4:7–12: "Let us love one another, because love is of God….If we love one another, God remains in us, and his love is brought to perfection in us."

⚭ Revelation 19:1, 5–9: "The wedding day of the Lamb has come, his bride has made herself ready."

Gospel Acclamation (Alleluia Verse)

(all from 1 John 4)

∞ "Everyone who loves is begotten of God..."

∞ "God is love..."

∞ "If we love one another, God remains in us..."

∞ "Whoever remains in love, remains in God..."

Gospel

∞ Matthew 5:1–12: The Beatitudes

∞ Matthew 5:13–16: "You are the light of the world."

∞ Matthew 7:21, 24–29: "Not everyone who says to me, 'Lord, Lord,' will enter the Kingdom of heaven, but only the one who does the will of my Father...."

∞ Matthew 19:3–6*: "What God has joined together, man must not separate."

∞ Matthew 22:35–40: "You shall love the Lord, your God, with all your heart...."

∞ Mark 10:6–9*: "They are no longer two but one flesh."

∞ John 2:1–11*: The Wedding at Cana

∞ John 15:9–12: "Love one another as I love you."

∞ John 15:12–16: "No one has greater love than this, to lay down one's life for one's friends."

∞ John 17:20–26: "I have given them the glory you gave me, so that they may be one, as we are one... that the love with which you loved me may be in them...."

Consent / Vows

∞ I, N., take you, N., to be my [wife/husband]. I promise to be true to you in good times and in bad, in sickness and in health. I will love you and honor you all the days of my life.

∞ I, N., take you, N., for my lawful [wife/husband], to have and to hold, from this day forward, for better, for worse, for richer, for poorer, in sickness and in health, to love and to cherish until death do us part.

∞ Answering "I do" to the presider's questions. (The questions asked differ if one of the persons is not baptized.)

Blessing of Rings

∞ "May the Lord bless these rings...as the sign of your love and fidelity."

∞ "Lord, bless these rings....Grant that those who wear them may always have a deep faith...."

∞ "Lord, bless and consecrate N. and N. in their love for each other. May these rings be a symbol of true faith in each other...."

Universal Prayer (Prayer of the Faithful)

These petitions should ask for blessing on the Church, peace in the world, the new couple, the sick, and the dead. There are sample sets from which to choose, or a couple may compose them in discussion with the presider, or he can prepare them himself.

Take this opportunity to invoke Mary and the saints. Some couples incorporate a "litany of the saints" hand-picked from among personal, family, and community favorites and patrons. This may be spoken, sung, or chanted.
See activity on page 46

Wedding Music

Consult with your parish and/or presider at least one month prior to the wedding. This often requires meeting separately with the music director or musicians about arrangements. There are a number of styles to choose from, including traditional, contemporary, classical, and more.

Processional _____

Gloria _____

Responsorial Psalm _____

Mass setting _____

∞ Alleluia _____

∞ Holy, Holy _____

∞ Memorial acclamation _____

∞ Great Amen _____

∞ Lamb of God _____

Offertory _____

Communion _____

Recessional _____

Other Song(s) (indicate title/composer and position within the ceremony)

_____

_____

_____

Wedding Vendors

The sacred nature of a church building and the wedding liturgy call for certain guidelines on the use of decorations, printed programs, and recording devices. Check with your presider or parish about regulations specific to your ceremony and location.

Planner / Coordinator _____

Photographer / Videographer _____

Florist _____

Program printer (stationery, calligraphy, etc.) _____

_____

Guest Accommodations _____

Baker / Caterer _____

_____

DJ / Reception Music _____

_____

_____

For Reflection and Discussion

1. Share with one another how you interpret your wedding day as being an act of worship.

2. How do you feel about the bride and groom processing in together?

3. Discuss the definition of "consent." How do you know if someone is really giving consent? Do you have examples of other times you gave consent?

4. Imagine the wedding has ended and you are married. What kind of (nuptial) blessing would you hope for from the Church?

5. Discuss the themes you each would like to have reflected in the readings at your wedding. Before you explored the list of options, did any scriptural passages come to mind?

My Thoughts

_____
_____
_____
_____
_____
_____
_____
_____
_____
_____
_____
_____
_____
_____
_____
_____
_____
_____

Communication in Marriage

David A. Smith, PhD

In this chapter...

- Communication is understanding, not just an expression.
- Communication is a skill that can be learned.
- Always seek and speak the truth.

L et's start with a wedding—the wedding at Cana—where Jesus began his public ministry and performed his first miracle (John 2:1–11). This Gospel story illustrates a fascinating bit of communication to contemplate. It begins, "the mother of Jesus was there. Jesus and his disciples were also invited…" (v. 1–2). This odd wording seems to suggest that Mary and Jesus were not at the wedding together. Mary learned of the lack of wine first, then had to find Jesus to tell him about it. The resulting dialogue is very brief:

The mother of Jesus said to him,
  "They have no wine."

[And] Jesus said to her,
  "Woman, how does your concern
  affect me? My hour has not yet come."

His mother said to the servers,
  "Do whatever he tells you."
                                        John 2:3–5

To make full sense of this exchange, we must go beyond the words. Jesus says no, but also implies that Mary's request was unreasonable. Apparently, he has no plans to launch his ministry or perform a miracle here and now. Mary doesn't ask Jesus for a simple or menial task. Had she, he may have happily complied. She asks for a great deal more and seems to know Jesus will see it her way, but not until after the human impulse to decline has passed his lips. Mary seems to be a step ahead of Jesus, but she had a head start.

Notice this. Neither one:

- needed to "talk it out."
- refuted a point or defended a position.
- became angry or defensive.
- invited another guest to stand as judge or jury.

Now wonder:

- How did they do it?
- Why is it so difficult for spouses to talk like that and to understand each other that way?
- How can our communication proceed so easily during conflict?

Communication Is a Skill

People sometimes object to change or resist adapting to new situations by claiming it should be "natural." They wrongly believe the problem is with the person, not the action, and that the only solution is to replace their spouse with another. **But the purpose of communication is not just to express yourself, but to produce understanding.** If what came naturally was effective, life's problems would no longer exist. So focusing on how you handle problems is better than focusing on their cause. Fortunately, it is easier to modify behaviors than personality "flaws."

Strong communication gets relationships through difficult patches. It takes time and practice, but the alternatives—marking a spouse or relationship as fundamentally flawed, irreconcilable, or defective—do not lead to marital improvement or happiness.

Mark an **H** for each sentence you have heard and an **S** for each sentence you have said. Mark a **B** for the words that both of you have said.

B I shouldn't have to tell him/her. (or, "It should go without saying.")

B Talking (or communication) should be natural.

H He/she should just know.

S He/she just doesn't get me.

H If he/she doesn't understand, it's not my fault.

S If he/she doesn't understand, he/she doesn't love me.

Effective Communication

Married couples are often able to predict exactly how their discussions will proceed—sometimes producing nearly word-for-word transcripts. There is no point in continuing these conversations. They can be frustrating and leave problems unresolved. More frequent communication only benefits when it is communicated well.

Practice doesn't make perfect; perfect practice makes perfect.

Couples in an unproductive rut need to make a change—where they talk, when they raise difficult topics, talking about the future rather than the past, etc. Any changes at all might move things forward.

Are You in a Rut?

1. What subjects do you discuss over and over?

2. What are your greatest disagreements or conflicts?

3. Can you quote a recent or recurring argument word for word? Where do things go wrong?

4. Are you guilty of wrongdoing or willing to concede or compromise?

5. What are some basic changes you can make right away?

You Want Me to Communicate Well All the Time?

Imagine walking down the sidewalk after a winter storm. You may first walk normally, but when you reach an icy stretch you cannot avoid, you slow down, lower your center of gravity, shuffle your feet, and focus on getting across the ice unharmed. Once you reach the other side, you speed back up, go back to your thoughts, and return to walking naturally.

Sometimes communicating well can be tiring or weird. Fortunately, for the most part, you are fine using your natural communication style. **But when the stakes are higher, when there is conflict, you need to focus and be careful.** If your natural way of communicating is not working, expect progress to come only from something that feels less natural.

Speak and Seek the Truth

In marital therapy, statements like the ones at right are described as cognitive distortions, because they involve the way one spouse thinks about the other and events in their marriage. **None of these statements is true**. Not only are they untrue, they are sure to produce a defensive response and are easily defeated by a counter-example. The catch? **The feelings behind the thought are true**. And feelings require more effort to express accurately.

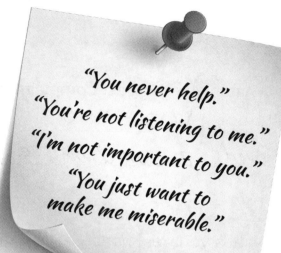

"You never help."
"You're not listening to me."
"I'm not important to you."
"You just want to make me miserable."

During a difficult conversation or when you are upset, take these steps. Examples are provided.

1. **Slow down. Hear your own words and identify your thoughts and feelings.**
   Example: "I'm angry because he never helps around the house."

2. **Ask yourself, "What is the truth?"**
   Example: "He helps out on occasion, but I want more help, especially after work when I'm trying to prepare dinner."

3. **Convert what you want into truthful, useful speech. Ask yourself:**
   a. **What can I say that is actually true?**
   b. **Is my mindset or language unproductive, extreme, or untruthful?**
   c. **Would my stance trigger a defensive response?**
   Example: "After work, I feel hungry, tired, and distracted. I could really use some help while I'm trying to get dinner on the table."

4. **Acknowledge what is good. Focus on the positive, describe what you want, and suggest solutions.**
   Example: "I appreciate all your help, especially on weekends. But on workdays, would you be willing to watch the kids or set the table while I finish making dinner?"

Now You Try It!

1. What is your biggest complaint about your spouse-to-be? _Doesn't listen_
Needs to slow down / Relax

2. What's your real concern? Is it really that big or bad? What are the facts? How do you feel?
Speaks/ignores (over) me   yes   irritated & unimportant!
Hyper-critical over little thing, no, condescended upon

3. Is anything exaggerated, untrue, or judgmental? Am I simply complaining, overreacting, or accusing?

4. How can I describe events, behaviors, and feelings so that they reflect the truth? What is right, and what do I want to change? How do I see this happening?

When you're both ready, share your prepared response, one partner at a time. Allow the listener to react and respond to your statements without interrupting, changing the subject, or halting the discussion. The problem-solving steps may help:

Problem-solving Steps

1. Identify/Clarify the problem. Avoid framing the problem too abstractly (for example, "There's a lack of trust.") It may not be true, and you may not disagree after all!

2. Brainstorm solutions. Put all your options on the table without judging.

3. Choose a solution. Pick one and try it out for a set time.

4. Evaluate its effectiveness. Skipping this step may delay a real resolution, and modifications may increase effectiveness and satisfaction.

Real Honesty

The conclusions people draw from poor communication can be detrimental. Extreme or immediate thoughts often have to be translated into the truth. If this is done habitually, spontaneous thoughts will eventually align with reality and result in better responses. You may see this as distorting or denying your feelings. It may even seem dishonest to think or feel one thing and say another. But reconsidering your thoughts—and even changing them—is a part of seeking the truth.

Consider racism. With time and experience, people with prejudices come to realize these thoughts are not true and resist expressing them. Through small but significant changes, erroneous thoughts cease and are replaced with the truth.

Head to Honest Ground.

Do You...

☐ Simply state your feelings?

☐ Say that you are frustrated or discouraged?

☐ Say what your spouse does?

☐ Describe your feelings?

☐ Distinguish fact from opinion?

or...

☐ State your interpretation of those feelings?

☐ Say why you feel that way (usually referencing an action or event)?

☐ Say what your spouse is (labeling, name-calling)?

☐ Relate someone else's feelings (perhaps presuming)?

☐ Treat opinions and personal observations as certain?

Truth is not measured by the intensity of a feeling, strength of a conviction, or repetition or popularity of a statement or belief. And expressing them and defending them as facts rather than theories is not honest. It requires humility to accept that some of the things you believe are not true. Most subjects involve another person (and therefore another perspective) with an equal claim to truth. And even when it seems to only affect you, there is always the person of Jesus, who is "the way and the truth and the life" (John 14:6).

Finally, **it is not especially honest to share every thought, feeling, and detail**. Instantly blurting everything out would be immodest and sound childlike. It's easy to find little dishonesties in phrases like, "you look fine" or "that's OK," and we say these things all the time. If you want a marriage in which both partners are not constantly hurt, we must choose our words, consider their effect, and avoid being careless.

Listening

This chapter has limited the discussion to "speaker" skills in contrast to "listener" skills. The roles of speaker and listener alternate frequently in marital discussions. Some label the roles "teacher" and "learner." For some people, the listener/learner skills seem especially difficult to acquire, perhaps because it is difficult to acknowledge and accept points we disagree with and listen attentively instead of formulating counterpoints for our rebuttal. Listening well, however, has surprising impact, and solves quite a few problems.

Speakers need to:

- stick to the topic.
- be concise.
- focus on being understood.

Date ___/___/___

Listeners need to:

- be overtly attentive.
- paraphrase the speaker. without adding or editorializing.
- focus on understanding.

Forgiveness and Reconciliation

One of the hardest things to say and hear is, "I'm sorry," and forgiveness is an essential aspect of marriage. The best way to increase mercy between spouses and within families is to practice it.

1. Reflect on the **Examination of Conscience** at right quietly and alone. Ask the Holy Spirit to help you see yourself as God sees you: imperfect yet lovable.

2. Select one or two actions or choices for which you need to seek forgiveness from your spouse-to-be.

3. Meet privately as a couple. Allow each person to both ask for and receive forgiveness.
   - [Name], I have injured or offended you by...
   - I love you and never desire to hurt you.
   - I beg your mercy and promise to do better.
   - I offer to make amends by...

4. Before the wedding, receive the **Sacrament of Reconciliation** together. While you won't hear each other's confessions, going together will provide mutual accountability and allow you to move forward toward marriage with a clean slate and a clean soul.

Examination of Conscience

† Do I put God first? Do I pray, ask God for help, and consider his ways and will in my daily life?

† Do I fill my mind with goodness, truth, and beauty? Do I speak well of God and treat holy things reverently? Do my words glorify God?

† Do I attend Mass on Sunday? Do I spend time drawing closer to God, enjoying creation, spiritual reading, or wholesome entertainment? Do I allow myself enough rest and relaxation?

† Do I honor my family and offer the care they need? Do I obey authority and respect my duties and obligations?

† Am I gentle and merciful? Do I injure others with my actions or choices? Do I care for my body and health? Do I get drunk or take harmful drugs or chemicals?

† Do I avoid impure influences and temptations? Do I support or engage in sinful sexual practices? Do I respect sex and procreation's rightful place within marriage?

† Do I seek permission and return everything I borrow? Do I give credit where credit is due? Do I "steal" time by cutting corners, arriving late, or leaving early?

† Am I honest? Do I lie for my own benefit or gain? Do I avoid gossip, defamation, and scandal?

† Do I promote fairness and justice? Do I avoid excess and greed? Do I waste resources?

For Reflection
and Discussion

1. Think back to an uncomfortable moment or conflict you have had with one another. What positive communication skills do you recall using? What skills could have been used better?

2. Share the good and bad communication skills you learned from your family. How were conflicts handled in the home—through withdrawal or isolation, giving more time to talk things out, shouting, judging, listening, respecting others' opinions?

3. Reflect on your own communication style. Consider body language, facial expression, tone of voice, sarcasm, humor, listening, and positive and negative affirmation of the other. Which ones do you think you use the most? Share your responses with each other.

4. What effective communication skills do you see in each other? Give an example.

5. Begin practicing careful communication skills and honest dialogue with your future spouse. Practice on the topics highlighted in this workbook and take time together to discuss matters of faith, family, love, and finances.

My Thoughts

_____

_____

_____

_____

_____

_____

_____

_____

_____

_____

_____

_____

_____

_____

_____

_____

_____

_____

_____

Family of Origin

Coleen Kelly Mast

In this chapter...

- Harmonizing differences while strengthening new connections
- The four temperaments
- Becoming our best selves together

Your Marriage

Each human came into being at conception and was created from love in order to partake in the love of God and share it with others. In short, **God is our origin and our destiny**. Marriage is a vocation, a particular expression of loving service, and on your wedding day, God entrusts to you your spouse, his unique work of art, to value and honor all the days of your life.

Spouses "bring" their families of origin into their marriages, consciously or not. Your "family of origin" is basically the family in which you grew up, had your basic needs met, and learned to communicate and manage emotions. It may also include your extended or adopted families or any community in which you discovered and developed your identity, key traits, and religious, social, or political views. **Each family, and each member, is unique in its genetics, habits, gifts, and customs**. Like parts of the body, God blessed them all with various gifts of the Holy Spirit.

Between you and your future spouse, there may be ethnic, racial, or religious backgrounds to harmonize. Often these differences are simple and attractive: new foods, new family customs and ties, new ways to relax. But there are challenges, too: compromising on holiday traditions, explaining one's faith to relatives, or learning a new social order or language. Whether you wish to change things from your childhood or repeat them, **this is your new life together, and you can make it what you want** in an effort to serve God better and together.

74

Patterns of Emotional Connection

Fundamental concerns to a new marriage often involve patterns of emotional connection that one or both partners had become accustomed to during childhood. These connections are what keep families intact, whether they are helpful or not.

Unhealthy Connections

- avoiding conflict
- competing against one another
- giving the silent treatment
- mistrusting others
- keeping secrets or withholding information
- criticizing constantly
- blaming others rather than admitting one's weaknesses

Healthy Connections

- cheerfully greeting one another
- letting one another always know of your whereabouts
- offering healthy physical affection and eye contact
- valuing family friendships
- working together on projects or housework
- praying and going to church together regularly
- always trying to solve differences to avoid major arguments
- making forgiveness a habit
- affirming one another

Marriage offers an opportunity to develop positive new habits. Consider the habits you acquired from childhood, and be sensitive to what you bring from your past, as well as the way your fiancé(e) responds to these habits. **Avoid using the excuse "that's just the way I am"** about a habit that can harm your love and care for one another. Harmful habits or traits and negative or false associations threaten the marriage and its call to equality and unity.

What Would You Do?

Bringing unaddressed issues into a marriage or setting unrealistic expectations on a spouse will likely create problems for both partners.

1. Sean is used to joking around in ways that hurt his wife's feelings. He thinks it's playful teasing and doesn't understand why she becomes upset.

2. Growing up, Isabella's home was full of sarcasm. Her husband notices that she uses it a lot when they talk together. Sometimes, he's not sure if and when she's being serious.

1. *If I were Sean's wife, I would...*

2. *If I were Isabella's husband, I would...*

Early in your marriage, become aware of the effects of your family of origin on your current behaviors. **Seek help and continued growth** through regular confession, spiritual direction and formation, professional counseling, marriage enrichment workshops, and knowing other successfully married couples.

3. Chris and Emily's marriage is built on the hope that hurts will go away on their own. He hates admitting he's wrong and assumes the problem is solved when the fighting ends. She'd rather wait for him to come around or do it her way, despite the consequences, than take the time to work out their disagreements.

3. *If I were Chris and Emily, I would...*

4. Jamie is accustomed to yelling, angry responses, and "short fuses." She admits to struggling to control her emotions but also needs to communicate her feelings and opinions.

4. *If I were Jamie's husband, I would...*

5. As a child, David had to meet his parents' high standards, and he still expects a lot from himself and others. Seeing his disappointment in minor mistakes, his wife feels undue pressure to please him, and she worries how he will respond when their children attempt and fail.

5. *If I were David's wife, I would...*

New Family Loyalty and the In-Laws

Successful marriages have partners who transfer their primary loyalty to their spouse from the day of the wedding onward. A couple who "becomes one" in marriage can still respect and remain loyal to both families of origin while making their new marriage and family a priority. If there is any conflict between your spouse and your parents, make your best effort to solve that conflict. Be careful never to criticize your spouse to your parents or siblings.

Three ways to grow in trust and loyalty:

1. *Time.* Offer any downtime to your spouse first. If you wish to make plans with your parents or siblings, ask your spouse and find out if he or she wishes to join you.

2. *Love and service.* Choosing to mow your mother's lawn when you have not taken out the garbage at your own house would not strengthen your marriage.

3. *Effort.* Direct your best time of day, greatest attention, and best work toward your marriage and new family. When it comes to loyalty and priorities, actions speak louder than words. Trust in God that your original family will respect your new life.

Harmonizing Different Temperaments

Just as a musical duet can be more melodious than a solo, harmonizing a couple's temperaments is beautiful. Most people are attracted to a person whose virtues they admire or even wish to acquire. You can learn from each other and balance each other out, especially when you see your spouse as a gift and enrichment rather than an annoyance or obstacle.

Your temperament is both a gift from God and an inherited trait from your ancestors. **No matter your temperament, you can choose to grow in virtue so that you become happier and have a happy family**. Growth in virtue and inner strength become your own "character" as you develop into a person of principles, utilizing your mind, emotions, and circumstances along with your will to do good. This good character is what made many people saints.

Understanding both of your temperaments can provide insights for both of you and make it easier to harmonize your strengths and weaknesses. Prior to the wedding, most couples have taken a personality test or premarital survey such as the Myers-Briggs, FOCCUS, or PREPARE/ENRICH inventory.

Also, many of the great saints, such as St. Thomas Aquinas and St. Francis de Sales, wrote about temperaments and how this knowledge can help in our spiritual growth. Marrying the opposite temperament can be good only if each spouse is willing to believe these traits are a gift to their marriage. As the years progress, one of the spouses can wrongly use the differences against the other, creating division instead of unity. If you decide you prefer yourself "your way" and try to justify your criticism rather than love the other as he or she is, you will miss the chance to help your partner feel secure and accepted.

Four Basic Temperaments

Hippocrates, an ancient Greek philosopher and physician, theorized there are four temperaments—each corresponding to a liquid inside the body.

❶ **The Sanguine** temperament was considered the liveliest due to rich, warm blood.

❷ **The Choleric** temperament indicated a leader or activist due to larger amounts of "chlor" or yellow bile.

❸ **The Melancholic** temperament indicated more serious moods from having black or darker blood or bile.

❹ **The Phlegmatic**, named after the word "phlegm," or thick, slow blood, was considered a person with a slower-moving temperament.

In simpler language, we can refer to the four temperaments as

❶ The **Talker** (Sanguine): the "Let's get together and have a good time" or socialite

❷ The **Doer** (Choleric): the "Let's get it done" or leader

❸ The **Thinker** (Melancholic): the "Let's get it right" or perfectionist

❹ The **Watcher** (Phlegmatic): the "Let's get along" or peacemaker

Of course, no one has just one temperament. We have blends, one dominant and others secondary. Furthermore, no temperament is best. **In a Christian marriage, we offer the richness of our strengths as a gift** to assist in our own growth and that of our spouse. We can also help one another avoid falling into problems from our temperamental weaknesses.

Humility—the truth of who we are before God—is the solution to appreciating your differences. Offer your gifts lovingly and patiently, behaving as your spouse's helpmate, not parent. Remember that your beloved is a gift from God, a gift that will help you see yourself, perfect yourself, and lead you to heaven. Your growth in virtue makes God's love visible to your spouse, and you become more attractive.

❶ Talkers are fun-loving and easygoing. They believe that people who take things too seriously need to "chill out," get a life, or go have some fun. They are bored when alone because they give and receive energy from others. They are outgoing, friendly, and expressive. Their moods change quickly, and they can easily forgive. On the negative side, they often exaggerate, are restless and weak-willed, and sometimes tardy or undependable. They do have a charisma that attracts others and makes them good salespersons.

❷ Doers are independent, strong-willed and make decisions easily. They are usually very practical, courageous, and have great vision and courage to make things happen. As they remain focused on their tasks, they can often be cold or unsympathetic, domineering, or sarcastic. They often struggle with pride and are "always right." Their confidence is attractive to others, and they are optimistic and successful leaders in their work.

❸ Thinkers are often great thinkers and naturally inclined to be more artistic or musical. They are gifted with analytical skills and usually have done well in school. They are conscientious and loyal, as well as self-sacrificing. They are often philosophical and like to think through things thoroughly. They can be touchy, self-centered, or impractical, or rigid and legalistic when someone is trying to get them to compromise. They have an idealism and intellect that make them great doctors or inventors.

❹ Watchers make good diplomats, teachers, or technicians. They are the most easygoing of the temperaments. Although more introverted, they often have a dry sense of humor that attracts people to them. They are loyal, dependable, practical, and likable. Since they'd rather be a spectator than a participant, they need motivation to get moving. They may shy away from making decisions but usually have good input if others are patient and affirming.

Temperament Chart

This chart classifies the general traits of each temperament.

1. In one color, circle the traits that describe you.
2. In another color, circle the traits that describe your fiancé(e).
3. Discuss instances in which you see your fiancé(e) display that particular trait.
4. Discuss how your strengths and weaknesses can create harmony in your life together.

	1. Sanguine	2. Choleric	3. Melancholic	4. Phlegmatic
General description	Likes to play Witty, easygoing, optimistic Avoids setting goals Likes to lead Extroverted, outspoken	Tends toward work rather than analysis Decisive, organized Prefers to lead Extroverted, outspoken	Goal-oriented Analytical Perfectionist Often introverted, soft-spoken, pessimistic	Likes to play but is pessimistic, introverted, soft-spoken Doesn't like to lead, analyze, or plan Likes peace and quiet Wants respect, low stress at work
Desires	Fun	Control	Perfection	Peace
When working with others	Needs attention, approval and affection from others Brings joy Likes to celebrate	Loyal, seeks appreciation Likes to control Wants praise, credit Wants to be involved	High standards and perfectionism create tension Will take tough jobs, let others do easy tasks Very critical because precision is key	Tends to be a homebody (at home, everything is under control) Will let others make decisions, is a good follower
Typically controls by	Charm	Threats of anger	Threats of moods	Procrastinating (avoids stress)

	1. Sanguine	2. Choleric	3. Melancholic	4. Phlegmatic
Strengths	Good company Team player Outgoing Responsive Warm, friendly Talkative Enthusiastic Compassionate	Natural leader Hard worker Strong-willed Independent Visionary Practical Productive Decisive	Hard worker Detail-oriented Gifted Analytical Aesthetic Self-sacrificing Industrious Self-disciplined	Likes tedious jobs Likes solitary work Calm, quiet Easygoing Dependable Objective Diplomatic Efficient
Weaknesses	Dislikes getting down to business Dislikes solitary activities Often tardy Undisciplined Emotionally unstable Unproductive Egocentric Exaggerates Irresponsible with money	Can be impatient, inconsiderate Tends to see others as means to goal May isolate self Cold, unemotional Self-sufficient Impetuous Domineering Unforgiving Sarcastic Angry Cruel	Unable to let go of projects until perfect Dislikes making mistakes Unforgiving Moody Self-centered Persecution-prone Revengeful Theoretical Unsociable Negative Critical	Slow starter Dislikes working under pressure Not self-motivated Unmotivated Procrastinator Selfish Stingy Self-protective Indecisive Fearful Worrier
How best to work with them	Put them to work with others Work alongside them	Use their initiatives Let them give input Pay attention to their strengths and contributions	When they list problems, they are trying to be helpful Take their objections seriously Be aware of their feelings	Lead the way Avoid sudden changes of plan Help them manage stress When they say no, they mean no
Saints and biblical examples	St. Peter Solomon Moses	St. Teresa of Ávila St. Ignatius of Loyola St. Francis of Assisi	St. Paul St. Thomas More St. Thérèse of Lisieux	Abraham St. Thomas Aquinas St. Bernadette Soubirous

Becoming Our Best Self: A Fitness Routine

Your body is not just a container for your soul. You are a whole human person, body and soul. As we offer ourselves in marriage, we need to be the best gift we can be in body, mind, and spirit.

For each kind of fitness listed below, your "workout" may include behaviors and activities you do alone or as a couple. Write down the "exercises" you already do, then add a new "target" that might further contribute to your overall health. Examples are provided.

	Goal	Example	Current Exercises:	Target:
Emotional	Goal: Understanding and managing feelings through healthy expression, not repression	Example: Refraining from profanity		
Social	Goal: Maintaining relationships that lead you to God and balancing them with your marital duties	Example: Attending friends' birthday parties		
Intellectual	Goal: Developing the mind and creativity; academic and artistic growth	Example: Completing college degree		
Mental	Goal: Focusing on positive thoughts; setting goals and following through	Example: Finalizing wedding guest list, being grateful for the budget and friends we have		
Physical	Goal: Maintaining your health and physical fitness; building strength, flexibility, and endurance	Example: Weekly Zumba class and softball game		
Spiritual	Goal: Increasing love for God and others each day; examining your life in light of faith and truth, leading to a greater understanding and practice of the faith	Example: Sharing a short prayer and wedding Bible passage at each weekend date		

You Are Not Alone

We celebrate marriage with festive showers, beautiful weddings, and delightful receptions. The guests receive the new couple with joy and pledge their support. This support does not end with the wedding gift. Your family and friends will console you in bad times and laugh with you in good times. **Married couples do well when they spend time with others who live the values of Christian marriage**. We all need the support and encouragement of a good example.

The Church is also here to support you in your marriage. Take advantage of opportunities for marriage enrichment in your area. Your priest, pastor, or parish staff can be contacted for any personal help. They look forward to meeting newly married couples at Mass.

Although many couples are already practicing their faith, the sacrament of marriage sometimes becomes a "call from God" to renew spiritual or religious practices that may have lapsed. The Church welcomes their return, and most parishes and dioceses have faith-formation classes, Bible studies, prayer groups, and preparation for the sacraments, including the Rite of Christian Initiation for Adults (RCIA).

At-home resources to grow in your faith include the Bible, the *Catechism,* and various Catholic media. If you do not have a Catholic Bible, make sure to put one on your wedding registry. When you have more serious problems, do not hesitate to seek professional help through Catholic counselors, therapists, and doctors. You must take care of your marriage and get the help you need before bigger problems arise. **Your marriage is valuable to God, to each of you, to the Church, and to society.**

TREASURE EVERY DAY!

For Reflection and Discussion

1. What were the strengths of your parent(s) and your upbringing? What were the weaknesses? What do you treasure most about your future spouse and your relationship?

2. How did your position in the family and childhood experiences help you become the person you are today? Discuss the differences and similarities you find.

3. What would you like to repeat in your marriage that you experienced in your childhood? What would you want to be different?

4. What differences and challenges in your relationship do you already observe? Do you do or say anything that hurts the feelings of your fiancé(e)? Why? Help each other gain understanding in these areas.

5. Share your responses to the following questions:

   a. How often do you see us visiting our respective families during our first year(s) of marriage?

   b. How do you prefer to divide and share household duties and chores?

   c. What kind(s) of vacations do you like? How often and for how long do you like to get away?

   d. Is there anything about your health, medical history, or family background that would help me understand you better or help you?

   e. What are your favorite resources for growing in the Catholic faith?

_____
_____
_____
_____
_____
_____
_____
_____
_____
_____
_____
_____
_____
_____
_____
_____
_____
_____
_____
_____

Money and Marriage

Phil Lenahan

In this chapter...

- Stewardship and generosity connect your faith and finances.
- Create a shared budget and financial plan.
- Savings and wealth creation are necessary.

Money management can become a critical and often unpleasant obstacle or threat to the balance and harmony of your marriage. Surveys continue to highlight money as one of the top three leading causes of marital conflict. As your lifelong journey begins, consider and discuss the course you will set for earning income, spending money, allocating assets, and saving for the future. Otherwise you may not reach your desired destination. The earlier you work together on a plan, the better off you will be.

Sadly, many people graduate from school without ever having been taught how to manage their resources. **Even those with financial skills must use them with another person who has an equal share in the outcomes and may have very different ideas.** Effective money management boils down to a few basics. This chapter touches on a number of issues that relate to your financial well-being. They fall into two essential aspects of managing money:

1. The link between faith and finances
2. The financial tools needed to manage your resources as a married couple

In addition to strengthening your financial well-being, these principles and practices will also strengthen your relationship with God and each other. Remember: Your marriage is not just the two of you. The marriage covenant includes God, who provides the guidance you need to fulfill your responsibilities.

Faith and Finances

Every couple needs to determine the financial principles they will follow. Will they follow worldly ways that focus on self and emphasize the accumulation of "stuff," or will they follow God's wisdom and focus on relationships and the things that matter more over the long haul?

If you are looking for clarity on how God wants you to treat your money, the Bible, the *Catechism*, and Church teaching have hundreds of references that paint a mosaic for how we should think about and act with money. They provide guidance on many topics, including:

- The importance of communication, honesty, and unity in marriage.
- The role generosity plays in growing your ability to love God and neighbor.
- The value of work and the importance of maintaining work-life balance.
- How having a plan helps you set priorities and reach your life's goals.
- An understanding that debt—improperly used—will keep you in financial bondage.
- How to understand saving and wealth creation through a Catholic lens.

The more closely you follow God's principles, the more complete and fulfilling your lives will be.

Listen to God's word on money

ISAIAH 55:2

"Why spend your **money** for what is not bread; your wages for what does not satisfy?"

Name three nonessential goods or services you buy regularly.

1. _____
2. _____
3. _____

1 TIMOTHY 6:10

"For the love of money is the root of all evils, and some people in their desire for it have strayed from the faith and have pierced themselves with many pains."

Name three things that make money management or stewardship difficult.

1. _____
2. _____
3. _____

SIRACH 29:9-11

"Because of the commandment, help the poor, and in their need, do not send them away empty-handed. Lose your money for relative or friend; do not hide it under a stone to rot. Dispose of your treasure according to the commandments of the Most High, and that will profit you more than the gold."

Name three ways you serve the poor and contribute to others' needs.

1. _____
2. _____
3. _____

MATTHEW 25:26-27

"So you knew that I harvest where I did not plant and gather where I did not scatter? Should you not then have put my **money** in the bank so that I could have got it back with interest on my return?"

Name three ways you can save, invest, or prepare for future expenses and emergencies.

1. _____
2. _____
3. _____

Stewardship

The principle upon which all others rest is that God is the Creator and ultimate owner of all that exists (Deuteronomy 10:14; Psalm 24:1). He has entrusted to us the responsibility of being his steward or manager. The *Catechism* describes us as "Stewards of Providence" (*CCC* 2404). These words capture the essence of our relationship with money. A steward's responsibility is to manage the resources entrusted to him or her in ways consistent with the desires and instructions of the owner. Once we understand this distinction—God is Creator and we are his stewards—our approach to finances in marriage has a more definitive direction. With this new knowledge, we can reset the course of our financial plan and end the argument over something that is not even ours. This insightful principle goes a long way toward creating financial peace in the home and allows the marriage to grow stronger.

The Importance of Generosity

Being grateful and generous are keys to fulfilling the great commandment of loving God and neighbor (Matthew 25:35–40). God wants us to be generous because he knows that is how we learn to keep our priorities straight (Malachi 3:7–10). But people tend to give out of what is left over rather than from their first fruits (Proverbs 3:9). According to a 2013 Barna Group study, 55 percent of American donors gave $500 or less per year to churches and nonprofits combined. While the universal Church does not require that the faithful tithe (contribute 10 percent), supporting the Church and her works is an obligation (*Canon* 222). Mother Teresa said, "Give until it hurts," and that is a good rule of thumb.

The Value of Work

Work makes up a large part of our lives, and its purpose goes well beyond earning a living and providing for your family's needs. Work provides an opportunity to participate in God's creative and redemptive plan for mankind. When you use your God-given talents, you develop yourself as a person of dignity and make a positive difference in this world.

Scripture and the *Catechism* make it clear that work is a duty (Proverbs 6:6–11; Colossians 3:23–24; *CCC* 2427). Saint Paul says, "If anyone was unwilling to work, neither should that one eat" (2 Thessalonians 3:10). Assuming we are able-bodied, we are expected to provide for ourselves and the common good. But learning to set balanced priorities, including those of faith and family, is as important as having a strong work ethic.

God makes it clear that we need to make our relationship with him a priority. And that takes time.

As much as you can, make your

We are to keep the Sabbath holy by...

- Resting and relaxing (Exodus 20:9–11; *CCC* 2184–2185);

- Participating at Mass and receiving the Eucharist when possible (*CCC* 2042, *Canon* 1247).

Sundays different from the rest of the week and special for your family. If your career or field demands that you work on Sundays, make sure you are meeting your religious obligations and taking time to recharge your batteries.

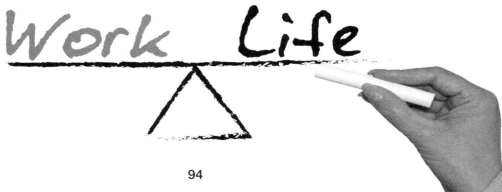

Keys to Financial Unity

By implementing the tips in this chapter, you will go a long way toward achieving the unity described in Genesis 2:24, which says, "a man leaves his father and his mother and cleaves to his wife, and they become one flesh." One key to this unity will be having Christ at the center of your relationship. Another key is to **maintain honesty and open lines of communication**. It's unfortunate, but there is a lack of honesty regarding money in far too many marriages. Sometimes this dishonesty takes the form of not being open about financial mistakes or of hiding problematic behavior. A marriage cannot withstand dishonesty. To enhance your communication and bring greater accountability, **set annual financial plans together**. Hold periodic meetings to review your financial progress, including a review of actual spending by category compared to your original plan.

The Importance of a Plan

If you want to reach your goals in life, you need a plan (Luke 14:28–30). People's financial lives are much more complex than a vacation; however, many put more time into planning trips than into planning their finances. As a result, they don't save, they incur unproductive debt, and they fail to align their resources with God's design.

One of the best gifts you can give yourselves is to create a budget for the first year of your married life. There are many types of budgeting systems, from envelopes to software programs. Whatever method you choose, the most important attribute is that it works for you. The latest and greatest program will not be effective if you do not use it.

An effective budget system offers a critical perspective of the "big picture" and helps you determine whether your income and expenses are balanced. Use an annual budget with year-to-date tracking. Income and expense transactions should be assigned categories. The system should allow you to review spending priorities by listing amounts spent in core categories as a percentage of gross income.

Prenuptial Agreements

Generally speaking, if you cannot combine your resources with your future spouse's "for better or worse," then you may want to discuss this as you prepare for joining yourselves in a covenantal marriage. In some cases, extenuating circumstances that warrant a prenuptial agreement may exist. For example, if one of you has dependents who rely on you for support and could be harmed in the event of a divorce, a "prenup" may be prudent. If your situation includes such complicating factors, seek the counsel of professional advisors and discuss the circumstances with the priest or deacon preparing you for marriage.

Fiancé

Fiancée

Signed in the presence of:

Witness

Guideline Budget

Use the following spending category percentages as a guideline for a family of four. Generally speaking, as income increases, the percentage for taxes increases, while percentages for general spending should decline, allowing for increases in charitable giving and savings. Since each situation is unique, these are only guidelines, but they do incorporate the principles of being a steward of Providence.

Category	Percentage of Income (guideline)	Percentage of Income (actual)
Charitable Giving (Tithe)	10%	
Saving	10%	
Taxes (Income and payroll related)	15%	
Education (Current)	3%	
Housing	30%	
Groceries	10%	
Transportation	9%	
Medical/Dental (excluding cost of insurance)	3%	
Insurance (Medical – assumes employer-based coverage; Life)	3%	
Debt Payments (unproductive debts)	0%	
Clothing	2%	
Entertainment and Recreation	3%	
Miscellaneous	2%	
Total	**100%**	

Dealing With Debt

For each type of debt listed below, each one of you should give an example of personal debts or expenses. Discuss the questions in each category and determine together whether a similar debt or expense would be accepted, modified, or avoided in your marriage.

Housing

Over the long term, real estate prices historically appreciate at a rate a bit higher than inflation. To borrow prudently for a home mortgage, then, can make perfect sense.

HIS: _____

_____

_____

HERS: _____

_____

_____

Ask:

$ Do we have enough cash to cover the expenses of a down payment, closing, and immediate repairs?

$ Do the mortgage payments, taxes, and ongoing costs of home maintenance fit into our current budget?

$ How much space and what features do we really need?

$ Do we intend to live in this location for an extended period?

$ What are our reasons for wanting to move here?

DEBT: Accept   Modify   Avoid

Credit cards

While using a credit card to make regular purchases is a practical tool, beware of using credit to borrow money for purchases that you cannot afford.

HIS: _____

_____

_____

HERS: _____

_____

_____

Ask:

$ Are these purchases part of our budget?

$ Do I pay the balance in full and on time every month?

$ When did I last make a credit-card purchase that appreciated in value?

DEBT: Accept   Modify   Avoid

Dealing With Debt *continued*

Cars, home equity, and other loans

New cars lose 15 percent or more of their value as soon as they are driven off the lot. The same is true for the majority of purchases using home equity loans.

HIS: _____
_____
_____

HERS: _____
_____
_____

Ask:

$ What will be the value of this purchase in five years?

$ Can I pay for this item in cash, even if that means waiting to buy? *Use the reserve fund methodology described later in the chapter.*

$ Are there more economical ways to meet my needs (buying used, repairing, or updating rather than re-placing)?

DEBT: Accept   Modify   Avoid

Education

The costs of higher education are great and rising. While a college degree still offers many benefits, the real value of your degree depends on many factors.

HIS: _____
_____
_____

HERS: _____
_____
_____

Ask:

$ What are my career prospects given my field and the existing job market? What is my expected salary range after graduation?

$ Is my program supporting me with essential skills, training, and experience? Does my school provide career counseling, services, or opportunities for internships?

$ Could I receive a similar education at a less- expen-sive school or through an apprenticeship, accelerat-ed, or part-time program?

$ Have I exhausted all my financial assistance op-tions, including grants and federal aid?

DEBT: Accept   Modify   Avoid

The Importance of Saving

In Genesis 41, Pharaoh appoints Joseph to successfully navigate Egypt through the challenges associated with seven years of famine. What did Joseph do? He set aside excess harvest during the seven years of plenty. Joseph's example provides a valuable lesson. While one might think it would be easier to save for the future if the Lord provided a dream as he did for Pharaoh, the reality is, **people *do know* of many future obligations yet fail to save for them:**

The temptation to avoid factoring in future expenditures to how we spend money today leads to debt. When we fail to save for these items, we end up borrowing to pay for them, and that borrowing will be an impediment to reaching our long-term financial goals. **An approach to saving called "Reserve Fund Management" will revolutionize your financial life.**

The concept is straightforward:

1. Make a list of the items you need based on a review of your life plans.

2. Build an appropriate level of savings into your annual spending plan in order to fund those future obligations.

- ▶ Emergency and rainy day

- ▶ Replacement vehicle

- ▶ Home improvement and repair

- ▶ Children's weddings

- ▶ College for children/ grandchildren

- ▶ Retirement

- ▶ Inheritance for children/ grandchildren

By building these savings into your current cash-flow plan, you actually set the money aside and only spend what is left over. This means you do not have as much money to spend today as you thought you did. Recognizing that and changing your habits accordingly is critical in making the reserve fund system work.

Reserve Fund Example

Let's say you have home-improvement projects that you would like to save for so you can complete them four years from now. You anticipate spending $25,000 on these improvements. You get paid every two weeks. The calculation goes like this:

Anticipated timing of purchase	4 years
Estimated purchase price	$25,000
Annual savings required	$6,250
Paycheck frequency	Bi-weekly (every two weeks or 26 per year)
Amount to be direct deposited into "Reserve Fund" every pay period	$240.38

By following this simple approach, you will save the $25,000 you need to make the home improvements in four years, and you will have done it without borrowing. This approach should be used for all expenditures that go beyond the one-year budget cycle.

Children and Education

You may think a discussion about the education of children is premature, but it is important to start thinking about one of the greatest responsibilities you will have: raising your children in the faith. This includes educating them during their formative years. The *Catechism* states: "The role of parents is of such importance that it is almost impossible to provide an adequate substitute. The right and the duty of parents to educate their children are primordial and inalienable" (*CCC* 2221).

Discuss how you anticipate fulfilling this responsibility (that is, Catholic education, homeschooling, public schools with supplemental faith formation) and how this great responsibility (and potentially great expense) fits into your financial priorities. If you both currently work, you can live on one income and save the entire second income. Not only will you learn the discipline of saving, you will find it much easier to have a parent stay home either full- or part-time when children arrive and to adjust your lifestyle when expenses increase and incomes decrease.

Living on One Income

While it is difficult for families to manage on one income, you may be surprised that in many situations, a second income may actually cost your family money. It is easy to think of gross income as the amount being added to the family coffers. In reality, many expenses are incurred to hold a job, including the cost of buying more convenience items due to a lack of time. When all of these costs are considered, you may find that you are working for less than minimum wage or losing money. By completing a simple income statement (see example at right) that summarizes the income and expenses associated with the second job, you can determine the net amount benefiting the family.

Income Statement

Gross income	$15,600
Minus	
Tithe	1,560
Taxes (estimate @ 30%)	4,680
Higher food costs	2,000
Auto costs	3,000
Child care	5,000
Clothing	500
Meals out	1,000
Total expenses	$17,740
Net loss	$2,140

Wealth Creation: A Responsibility

While saving and the creation of wealth are related, they are distinct issues. **Catholics have a responsibility to create wealth.** The *Catechism* says, "The ownership of any property makes its holder a steward of Providence, with the task of making it fruitful and communicating its benefits to others, first of all his family" (*CCC* 2404).

In the parable of the talents (Matthew 25:14–30) the two servants who grow their talents are commended and given more. The servant who buries his talent is chastised. The biblical message is clear: **The Lord wants your gifts to grow** so they may better provide for your family and help others.

Wealth creation usually results from steadily saving and investing a portion of one's salary over a long period of time. In this case, the key is compound earnings. To obtain its benefits, you need to invest consistently from an early age and obtain a reasonable rate of return for the level of risk appropriate for you.

Wealth can be a source of great good, but it also has the potential for harm. Here, as ever, God's admonitions about attachments to money remain true. Consider Mark 8:36: "For what does it profit a man, to gain the whole world and forfeit his life?" **When it comes to wealth, the question is not whether (or how far) to allow it to grow; it is how and why.** Use your talents to create wealth, yet remain detached from it. Use your money to please the Lord and to fulfill your responsibilities. *Don't fall into the trap of "having" rather than "being."*

Quick Tips

- Keep your wedding and honeymoon expenses reasonable and within your means.

- Before you marry, consider which financial planning strategies you want to use and who will handle financial chores such as preparing budgets, paying bills, and tracking activity. Make sure the one responsible has the skills and time to do the job well.

- How you organize your finances should facilitate financial unity. That means having a combined financial plan even if there are valid reasons to hold some assets separately.

- Prioritize your charitable giving first and your savings second. Live on the remainder.

- Don't rush in to buying a house. Renting provides the flexibility you need until your situation is sufficiently stable to purchase a home. Because of the cost of completing a buy/sell cycle (typically over 10 percent of the property's value), you will want to be confident you can stay in a home for at least five to seven years before making a commitment. Proverbs 24:27 provides great wisdom: "Complete your outdoor tasks, and arrange your work in the field; afterward you can build your house."

By becoming more effective stewards of Providence, your love for the Lord and each other will grow each day. You will use the resources entrusted to you in ways that are pleasing to him and good for you. More resources are included at the end of this chapter.

For Reflection
and Discussion

1. Reflect on the impact your family and upbringing has had on your attitude toward money. How did your parent(s) treat, discuss, and manage money?

2. How does your faith impact your financial values and habits? Share an example or two with each other.

3. List five reasons for living on a budget. Are there any good reasons for not having one? What gets in the way of creating and living on a budget?

4. List your five most important financial goals and the obstacles impeding your reaching them. What steps can you take to eliminate or reduce these obstacles?

5. What are your current assets and liabilities? Before the wedding, list your combined accounts, holdings, and debts. This is the first step in building your first-year budget.

_____

_____

_____

_____

_____

_____

_____

_____

_____

_____

_____

_____

_____

_____

_____

_____

_____

_____

_____

_____

Sample Balance Sheet

Also available at liguori.org/marriage

Description	Current Year	Prior Year
Assets		
Cash and Cash Equivalents		
Cash on Hand	100	100
Cash - Checking	1,100	1,100
Cash - Money Market	-	-
Cash - Other	-	-
Total Cash and Cash Equivalents	1,200	1,200
Invested Assets		
Certificates of Deposit	-	-
Brokerage Accounts	-	-
Retirement Plans	12,000	11,000
Business Investment	-	-
Total Invested Assets	12,000	11,000
Use Assets		
House	250,000	240,000
Autos	15,000	17,000
Other	10,000	10,000
Total Use Assets	275,000	267,000
Total Assets	**288,200**	**279,200**
Liabilities		
Mortgage and Home Equity Loans	200,000	203,000
Auto Loans	10,000	12,000
Credit Cards and Installment Loans	10,000	7,000
Student Loans	-	-
Business Debt	-	-
Other (Loans: Family and Friends; Retirement Plans; Life Insurance)	-	-
Total Liabilities	**220,000**	**222,000**
Net Worth	**68,200**	**57,200**

Sample Budget

Also available at liguori.org/marriage

Account Description	ACTUAL Income/Expenses	ACTUAL Annual %	GUIDELINE Budget	GUIDELINE Budget %
Gross Income	80,000	100%	80,000	100%
Salary	75,000			
Bonus	2,000			
Interest	-			
Dividends	-			
Retirement Plan	-			
Other	3,000			
Tithe/Giving	800	1%	8,000	10%
Deductible	800			
Non-deductible	-			
Children Tuition	-			
Taxes	13,600	17%	12,000	15%
Federal Income	5,000			
State Income	2,000			
Social Security	5,000			
Medicare	1,200			
State Disability	400			
Current Education	200	0%	800	1%
Tuition (See tithe)	-			
Supplies	200			
Day Care	-			
Other	-			
Savings	-	0%	7,200	9%
Emergency and Rainy Day	-			
Future Education	-			
Retirement Plan	-			
Housing and Home Expenses	30,400	38%	24,800	31%
Mortgage/Rent	18,000			
Insurance	800			
Taxes	3,000			

►

Sample Budget *continued*

Also available at liguori.org/marriage

Account Description	ACTUAL Income/Expenses	ACTUAL Annual %	GUIDELINE Budget	GUIDELINE Budget %
Electricity	1,000			
Gas	900			
Water	800			
Gardening	800			
Housecleaning	-			
Telephone	1,000			
Maintenance	1,500			
Pest Control	400			
Association Dues	-			
Bottled Water	-			
Postage	200			
Miscellaneous	-			
Improvements	2,000			
Groceries	11,200	14%	8,800	11%
Transportation	7,700	10%	8,000	10%
Payment/Replacement Savings	3,600			
Gas/Oil	2,000			
Insurance	800			
License/Taxes	300			
Maintenance/Repair	1,000			
Medical Expenses	2,400	3%	2,400	3%
Doctor	1,500			
Dentist	500			
Prescriptions	400			
Other	-			
Insurance	2,400	3%	2,400	3%
Medical	900			
Life	1,500			
Disability	-			
Debt Payments	3,500	4%	-	0%

▶

Sample Budget *continued*

Also available at liguori.org/marriage

	ACTUAL	ACTUAL	GUIDELINE	GUIDELINE
Account Description	Income/Expenses	Annual %	Budget	Budget %
Credit Card	3,500			
Loans and Notes	-			
Other	-			
Clothing	4,000	5%	1,600	2%
Entertainment/Recreation	5,100	6%	2,400	3%
Eating Out	3,300			
Babysitting	-			
Cable/Satellite/Movies	800			
Allowances	-			
Activities	-			
Vacation	1,000			
Work-Related	-	0%	-	0%
Education/Dues	-			
Internet/Phone	-			
Other	-			
Miscellaneous	3,200	4%	1,600	2%
Beauty/Barber/Cosmetics	800			
Laundry	200			
Subscriptions	200			
Holiday/Gifts	1,700			
Accounting/Legal	100			
Veterinarian/Animals	200			
Summary of Inc./Exp.				
Total Income	80,000	100%	80,000	100%
Total Expenses	84,500	106%	80,000	100%
Income Over/(Under) Exp.	(4,500)	-6%	-	0%

Intimacy

Bridget Brennan

In this chapter...

- Intimacy reflects the Trinity.
- Qualities and rewards of true intimacy
- Meeting wants, needs, and requirements

In today's world, the word *intimacy* means different things to different people. Sales people are told to be "intimate" with their customers. Relationships between lovers as well as mother and newborn are defined as "intimate." There are countless articles and suggestions for creating an "intimate" environment. As a word, it is often used out of context or overused.

So what is intimacy? Its essence is rooted in these words of Jesus: "Holy Father, keep them in your name...so that they may be one just as we are" (John 17:11). **Our call to intimacy, to oneness with another is to be as profound as the union of the Trinity**. As we noted earlier, the marriage covenant exists not only between the wife and husband; God shares in their unity.

The triune God—one in three distinct persons—is love and the essence of intimacy. As people created in God's image, we require love and relationship for sustenance and survival. Over time, day by day, in emotionally healthy relationships, we are graced with mirroring the Trinity in our own lives and marriages. This occurs very slowly, at times imperceptibly, and it builds on nature—**which means that each of us has to learn the little ways, the simple ways, that we can build intimacy** between a husband and wife. Sadly, we too often destroy intimacy; we take it for granted and forget our love needs nurturing and nourishment.

Qualities of Intimacy

- *Intimacy is real.* We sense it in varying degrees and often know when we don't have it. Like the sun on a cloudy or rainy day, we are aware of its absence.

- *Intimacy is intangible.* It's a mystery but not magical.

The qualities and nature of intimacy in your marriage may shift as you move and grow through various stages and cycles of life, but the following qualities are essential for every couple in every marital stage.

1. **Wholeness / Holiness**
   God invites us, calls each person, to a wholeness/holiness in Christ. "In Him we live and move and have our being" (Acts 17:28). If we are not emotionally healthy we won't be able to experience that wholeness in Christ or that intimacy with our spouse. In other words, if it is not healthy, it's not holy. Intimacy is holiness.

2. **Mutual Desire**
   The desire to hold each other and be held is a longing that grows as the couple grows in love. As each one sorts out selfish desires, the desire to love becomes more mutual and they find more satisfaction in their relationship.

3. **Trust**
   Trust is essential to a successful marriage. Each spouse must believe the other to be reliable, honest, faithful, authentic, committed to working together, and willing to learn what mutuality means in building a relationship of love. Each spouse must feel completely safe with the other.

4. **Honesty**
   Honesty involves much more than not telling lies. Honesty is revealing the truth about feelings and intentions. It allows a wife and her husband to share their feelings even if they know the other may not like to hear those feelings. Intimacy flourishes when a couple risks being completely honest with each other.

5. **Fidelity**
   The marriage covenant and vows call spouses to be faithful to one another in Christ. Husbands and wives need to remain faithful to the call of marriage that God has given them. This means living a life of integrity. Choosing not to engage in pornography, extramarital flirting or affairs, unhealthy relationships, vulgar language, and any kind of abuse are some examples.

6. **Humor**
   There are jokes, anecdotes that are privately shared between the wife and husband. A shared sense of humor claims the relationship is their own. If they tried to explain the joke to others, the humor would likely be lost on them.

Getting to Know You

1. Draw a line from each trait of intimacy to the one who embraces it the most. If you both equally possess a given trait, draw two lines—one to each person. Be prepared to cite a specific example of how that trait is expressed.

2. Circle three to five traits that you deem most essential to your marriage. Compare lists with your future spouse.

3. Identify any intimacy strengths or gaps in your relationship. (Both partners naming the other for the same trait may signal a gap.) For each gap, determine a behavior or activity that might foster that quality. Seek help if needed.

Physical Affection / Closeness
Support / Encouragement
Sharing / Expressing Self
Honesty
Reaching out to Connect
Peacemaking
Forgiveness (requesting)
Forgiveness (offering)
Vulnerability
Accommodation / Compromise
Fidelity
Desire for the Other
Giving / Sharing of Joy, Pleasure
Holiness / Integrity
Commitment (to the marriage)

Intimacy strengths: _____

Intimacy gaps: _____

Proposed exercise(s) to improve intimacy: _____

Red Flags for False Intimacy

1. Unhealthy Dependency

Intimacy is not infatuation or romanticized friendship.
Though often mistaken for intimacy, these are usually
based on an inappropriate neediness for the other.
"I can't live without you" is a red flag. Each of us is
unique, and each of us must have a sense of autonomy
before we can enter into a committed relationship.
**We cannot give ourselves to another unless we have
a sense of our own self, our own self-worth.** If a spouse
is not emotionally independent, the marriage will most likely
become dysfunctional and bear no good fruit of intimacy.

2. Isolation

Isolation shuts others out. In marriage, marital love and
monogamy are exclusive, but being isolated from all
others, especially extended family, can be dangerous.
We live in community and in communion with the Church,
God's body, with many parts and members. Isolation
can be a factor in finding ourselves in—perhaps a sign of—
a controlling, unhealthy relationship.

3. Possessiveness

Possessiveness creates unhealthy barriers. Love never
possesses the other. Rather, true intimacy frees us to be
with and for others as long as we maintain parameters,
set priorities, and know that our spouse and children take
priority over other commitments. Loved unconditionally,
we are energized to move beyond ourselves. The
marriage covenant is the foundation for mission and
service to others.

Fears Hinder Growth in Intimacy

All of us harbor some degree of hidden fear, possibly caused by past events. Whatever the cause or reason, fears influence our attitudes, behaviors, and reactions to certain experiences.

Some common fears are:

- Rejection
- Loss
- Failure
- Abandonment
- Possession (by another)

Specific fears and their relative degree(s) vary from person to person. When we risk being in an intimate relationship, our vulnerability surfaces. In this vulnerable state, our sensitivity is heightened, and we become more alert to these fears as we strive to grow in intimacy.

The maxim is, "Either you control your fears or your fears control you." **Husbands and wives need to face their fears together** and try to understand how a particular fear hinders them from growing in intimacy. For example, if he has a fear of being rejected, he will be very cautious and slow in risking deep intimacy. His wife may interpret his actions or words as deliberately distancing himself or withdrawal. The same would be true if, for example, the wife fears being possessed or isolated from others by her husband. Her actions may then be guarded and defensive, which will make growing in intimacy very difficult.

A grace of marital love is its power to be a source of healing for each spouse as they face their fears and grow as individuals and in unity with one another. Allow Scripture to have the final word:

> "There is no fear in love, but perfect love drives out fear…"
>
> 1 John 4:18

Turning Toward Each Other

In his bestselling book, *The Seven Principles for Making Marriage Work*, noted therapist John M. Gottman, PhD, counsels couples to "turn toward each other instead of away." He warns against getting caught up in daily activities and responsibilities and taking our spouse for granted, which erodes intimacy over time.

Answer the following questions for yourself. You will share responses at the end.

1 *I feel most romantic, grateful for, and connected to my spouse...*
- ☐ In the morning
- ☐ Midday
- ☐ At night
- ☐ At special times / On certain dates (please specify):

  _____
- ☐ Whenever we're together
- ☐ During certain activities (please specify):

  _____
- ☐ When I...
- ☐ When my spouse...
- ☐ When I see, hear, or think about...

2 *I'm most likely to offer (and/or be open to receiving) physical affection...*
- ☐ In the morning
- ☐ Midday
- ☐ At night
- ☐ At special times / On certain dates (please specify):

  _____
- ☐ Whenever we're alone
- ☐ During certain activities (please specify):

  _____
- ☐ When I...
- ☐ When my spouse...
- ☐ When I see, hear, or think about...

3 *I'm most open to speaking with and listening to my spouse...*
- ☐ In the morning
- ☐ Midday
- ☐ At night
- ☐ Whenever we're alone
- ☐ During a date or special outing / activity
- ☐ When we're physically close or touching
- ☐ After showing physical affection or connection

Turning Toward Each Other *continued*

4 I tend to share information...
- ☐ In person
- ☐ In a phone call
- ☐ In a long letter
- ☐ In a quick message
- ☐ Through a third party
- ☐ Through physical and emotional cues
- ☐ I keep things to myself.

5 I prefer to receive information...
- ☐ In person
- ☐ In a phone call
- ☐ In a long letter
- ☐ In a quick message
- ☐ Through a third party
- ☐ Through physical and emotional cues
- ☐ I'd rather not know certain things.

6 I prefer to process information... (Check all that apply.)
- ☐ In small bits
- ☐ As a whole
- ☐ Gradually over time
- ☐ Once and for good
- ☐ Alone
- ☐ With others
- ☐ With few distractions
- ☐ While keeping busy

7 My biggest distractions and obstacles are... (Check all that apply.)
- ☐ Jobs / career
- ☐ Children / family
- ☐ Hobbies / interests
- ☐ Media / entertainment
- ☐ Cultural, religious, or personal differences
- ☐ Personal challenges, traumas, or addictions
- ☐ Lies / secrets / sin
- ☐ Fears / lack of trust
- ☐ Doubts, indifference, or lack of commitment to marriage

8 I encourage and support my spouse by... _____

9 My spouse can encourage and support me best by... _____

10 We best turn toward each other... _____

11 We turn away from each other... _____

Wants, Needs, and Requirements

Everyone has basic needs and requirements for being content with life. When these things go unmet, an individual often becomes unhappy, restless, sometimes angry, and depressed. In marriage, spouses need to recognize and share with one another their wants, needs, and requirements. Keep in mind: No spouse is responsible for identifying and fulfilling every need of the other, though often he or she can be part of the solution. In any case, listening to and respecting each other in these areas will greatly aid a couple's growth in intimacy.

Wants

Wants provide pleasure and enjoyment. They are often marketed as things or experiences: the latest technological device; the leading fashion or trend; a vacation at a fancy resort. Wants are changeable, and they are easily negotiated. For instance, "I may think I want a large house when we marry, but eventually I find myself happy with the smaller house that we have and can afford. I may think I want a more expensive car, but looking at the budget I am OK with my more modest car that is reliable." Most married couples find ways to compromise their wants—at least some of them—and/or delay gratification.

Needs

Needs are more easily recognized and understood when they are not being met. An unmet need can escalate quickly to an "issue." The ensuing conversation usually begins with, "We need to talk." Some emotional and functional needs are influenced by personality type. For example, some temperaments like to plan ahead and have a checklist. For a more spontaneous personality, this planning can cause stress or feel controlling. Differences like these can be resolved through patience and communication. When spouses open up and identify the problem exactly, they can begin to solve the problem.

Requirements

Requirements are what each of us needs in order to remain balanced and composed. A relationship will not last if our requirements are not being met. Though an individual's requirements are non-negotiable, they are not unreasonable demands. Couples should discuss, if not begin to address, requirements with one another prior to becoming engaged. Some requirements can be addressed more easily before marriage, children, or relocation.

Deal Breakers

Make a list of your wants, needs, and requirements. Share and discuss your lists with your spouse-to-be. This is where compromise can work.

Example: A husband required a certain amount of time alone each day. Together the couple realized he has the right and responsibility to carve out time for himself. She understands this is a struggle for him and encourages him to try different ways of meeting his "alone time" within their schedule.

Wants	Him	Her
Are…		
Currently met with/by… (if unmet, write n/a)		
Suggested solutions		

Needs	Him	Her
Are…		
Currently met with/by… (if unmet, write n/a)		
Suggested solutions		

Requirements	Him	Her
Are…		
Currently met with/by… (if unmet, write n/a)		
Suggested solutions		

1 Wholeness

2 Freedom

3 Worth and Meaning

4 Courage

5 Joy

Rewards of Intimacy

Wholeness
The union of a married couple grounds both in the knowledge of not only where they belong but also with whom. Husband and wife reach wholeness together. The oneness of marriage is actually what they become (Genesis 2:24). This union is the unbreakable bond of the marriage covenant.

Freedom
True marital intimacy brings the freedom to love unconditionally and to risk total self-giving in the relationship. That unconditional love is the foundation for freedom. Love is given and received in marital intimacy without expecting the other to be any different.

Worth and Meaning
Love and intimacy provide purpose to married life. Marriage takes attention, focused energy, and commitment—some simply call it "work." We are continuously assailed with distractions and obstacles to intimacy. Likewise, infidelity of any sort damages the couple's intimacy, threatens the relationship's meaning and worth, and therefore is not acceptable.

Courage
As husband and wife experience intimacy in their love, God empowers each one to be self-confident and free to live their lives as disciples, to be authentic and walk in the truth, to courageously reflect Gospel values.

Joy
Joy is probably the greatest reward of intimacy. We are each created for joy, and Jesus came into our world to restore and reclaim that complete joy which is the fruit of love (John 15:11)

A Broader View of Intimacy

Sexual intimacy is an essential element of married love and life, but needs to be part of a larger intimate relationship. Sexual intimacy spills over from the bedroom into intimacy with your spouse in other ways: reorganizing a closet together, attending prenatal classes during pregnancy, walking through the park, or sharing a movie. Conversely, building up these moments outside of the bedroom each day contributes to romance and enhances sexual intimacy. **Sexual intimacy is a reflection of the spouses' attention, care, and respect shown in all elements of their married life.**

Saint Paul's poetic discourse on love (1 Corinthians 13) doesn't refer specifically to marital intimacy, but it expresses the deep, mutual respect and self-giving that is sacramental love. Rudeness, quick tempers, selfishness, and holding grudges diminish intimacy. Patience, honesty, forgiveness, and endless hope strengthen intimacy. These attributes may not be easy at times, but as St. Paul says, "Love never fails" (v. 8).

The Five Love Languages

Not uncommonly, spouses have an inaccurate idea of how the other wants to be loved. Without a clear understanding of what "loving your spouse" means to one another, the couple risks being in a marriage where one of them feels essentially unloved. Certainly this is an unintended consequence, but that is how the behavior has been translated.

Through decades of counseling and pastoring married couples, Gary Chapman, PhD, has developed "The Five Love Languages." He believes that each individual has his or her own "love language," or way by which she or he wants (and sometimes needs) to be loved and to show love. In his book of the same title, Chapman explains that each of us has a favorite or most-often-used way of loving and needing to be loved:

1. Words of Affirmation
2. Quality Time
3. Receiving Gifts
4. Acts of Service
5. Physical Touch

To discover which love language each person prefers and uses, it would be valuable for couples to read Chapman's *The Five Love Languages* together.

The Perfect Date

Consider the factors that go into planning a date:

- Shared activities that engage each partner's preferences and style, and allow for closeness and unity;

- An atmosphere of trust, desire, and joy (often through laughter);

- Timing that provides for needs, meaningful attention, and honest communications.

Below, describe the "perfect" date for you and your spouse. Make sure it accounts for both of your "love languages" and ideas on romance and intimacy. If you do, you will be eager to schedule it.

_____

_____

_____

_____

_____

_____

_____

_____

_____

_____

_____

_____

For Reflection and Discussion

1. How have you experienced intimacy in your relationship thus far? Share a few examples with one another.

2. Reflect on your call to mirror the triune love of God in your marriage. Discuss what appeals to you about this image of intimacy and what it will mean for your relationship.

3. How accepting of—or resistant to—emotional intimacy are you? What reasons or experiences can you give to explain your position? How can you, as a couple, work to achieve a comfortable balance of autonomy and intimacy in your marriage?

4. Reflect on your fears. Share one with your future spouse, and together explore ways that you can support each other in gradually letting go of those fears.

5. Review the sidebar on the "five love languages." Which love language(s) do you identify in yourself? In your future spouse?

My Thoughts

_____
_____
_____
_____
_____
_____
_____
_____
_____
_____
_____
_____
_____
_____
_____
_____
_____
_____
_____

Sexuality

Charles E. Bouchard, OP

In this chapter...

- God's design for sex and sexuality
- The dual purpose of intercourse
- The morality of sexual acts and practices

What is sex? This question has a variety of answers. "Sex" can refer to biological gender, that is, whether each of us is genetically and biologically a male or female. In this sense, sex is a biological fact, verifiable by scientific research and not open to dispute. This sex-identity gives an individual a certain set of tools, including distinctive sexual parts and a brain (which has been described as the biggest sexual organ). These tools enable us to do certain things, and the evaluation of what we do with these tools is the basis of sexual morality.

While our sexual organs are the physical manifestation of our sex, sexuality is the social manifestation of it. **Sexuality is rooted in gender**, but it includes the attitudes, emotions, cultural expectations, roles, and subjective experiences that occur when we interact with the world. We gradually learn to relate to others as sexual beings; through the lens of our gender and experiences, we acquire a unique "sexual language." Although there are some typically "male" and "female" ways of relating to others, we have a wide repertoire of capabilities. Men can be tender and affirming, and women can be decisive and analytical.

"Sex" also refers to what we do physically with our gender tools, as when we "have sex." Sexual relations and acts engage our sexual selves—biological, genetic, emotional, and social—in a dramatic and profound way. This makes sex a very powerful drive, second only to our desires for food and water. **"Having sex" is a deep "self-speaking" that comes from the very core of who we are.** Although the Church is often criticized for devoting too much attention to matters of sex, there is good reason. It is unlike any other kind of human exchange, with an enormous power for good and evil. This is why it raises so many important moral questions.

130

A Theology of the Body

The human body—its physical makeup, meaning, and purpose—comes from God and affects how we understand and interact with faith. Many understandings of the body and sexuality are not compatible with Scripture or the message of Jesus. For instance, some see the body as just a collection of molecules with no transcendent or spiritual dimension. This secular viewpoint has close cousins in consumerism, totalitarianism, and various kinds of slavery and human subjection. Others may even reject the body as evil or corrupt and seek a "spiritual" existence that seeks to punish or neglect the body. Both of these extremes have surfaced repeatedly throughout history, yet neither of them is consistent with our tradition.

In response to these views, Pope St. John Paul II delivered a "theology of the body" in a series of Vatican audiences. Here is a rough summary:

1. **We are created in the image of God** and as free beings who can choose to cooperate with and uniquely express God's presence and truth through our identities and choices.

2. **Man was originally alone, but found companionship** in the first woman who was his equal, helpmate, and partner in creating.

3. Despite sin, we are called back to God through Jesus. **Marriage imitates the union of Christ to his Church** (Ephesians 5), which is bodily, loving, permanent, and redemptive.

4. The body is relational. **We do not achieve holiness *in spite of* our bodily relationships, but *by means of* them.** Intercourse within marriage is the purest example of this holy relationality.

5. **Marriage, *and the marital act itself*, is sacramental**: "The body, and it alone, is capable of making visible what is invisible: the spiritual and the divine" (*Man Enters the World as a Subject of Truth and Love*; February 20, 1980).

6. **Marriage foreshadows the kingdom of God**, where there is no division or disintegration.

Therefore, a fully human, loving marital act involves not just two people, but three: the husband, the wife, *and* God. Just as the other sacraments have tangible means by which grace is present (bread, water, oil), so in marriage, the physical (sexual) relationship that flows from the covenant is the tangible means of grace. Sexual pleasure in marriage can actually be a sign of God's presence.

Getting to Know You

The adjectives below can describe both men and women. Give an example of how you fit each trait in the column for your gender, then give an example of each for your fiancé(e).

How Are You...?	He is...	She is...
Attractive		
Generous		
Loving		
Sexy		
Strong		
Supportive		

Share and discuss your responses. What does it mean to be a husband or a wife, a man or woman of God? How does your gender and God-given traits make you specially suited to certain acts, ministries, and duties of marriage?

The Purpose of Intercourse

Some people have sex for money; some to express love. Some want to procreate; others merely seek self-satisfaction. **The Catholic tradition sees two noble aims for sexual activity: procreation and mutual love (unity).** In fact, these two aspects of intercourse, while distinct, are inseparable. The fullest expression of human sexuality is a freely chosen sexual encounter with a married partner that conveys love and commitment *along with* an openness to the possibility of new life. To the extent that one or both of these dimensions are lacking, the sexual act falls short of moral perfection and its full potential.

Sexual morality is evaluated in terms of whether a given act contributes to the good of the individuals and brings unity with each other and with God, or whether it works against those things, as well as the person's reasons and intentions. Sex can be an authentic "self-speaking" or a lie; it can be a generous gift or a hurtful assault. A major goal of marriage is to work toward a sexuality that deepens the spouses' love and makes their covenant a sign of God's self-giving love.

Sex deepens the love of the spouses and transforms their covenant into a radiant sign of God's love in the world.

Virtuous sexual acts:

- honor the dignity of the human person.
- express Christian love as modeled by Jesus.
- demonstrate integrity and authentic communication.
- contribute to wholeness, true happiness, and fulfillment.

Immoral sexual acts:

- debase a person, object, group, or sexuality as designed by God.
- create division between partners, families, and a person's own values and actions.
- deceive another or lead him or her into sin.
- hinder or prevent free will, true consent, or fidelity.

Sexual Feelings

Complete each statement below with the word or words from the box that best express your current feelings.

Afraid	Aroused	Ashamed	Comfortable
Excited	Holy	Impatient	Indifferent
Loved / Loving	Proud	Self-conscious	Used

1. When I think about appearing naked in front of my spouse-to-be, I feel…

_____

_____

2. When I think about flirting and expressing my sexuality with him/her, I feel…

_____

_____

3. When I think about having sex with my spouse-to-be, I feel…

_____

_____

4. When I think about conceiving and/or bearing children with my him/her, I feel…

_____

_____

Share and compare your responses with each other. Are your attitudes generally healthy and positive? Do they reflect a growing trust and desire for unity? Are there any areas of great difference or concern?

Sexual Practices in Marriage

Because marriage is the union of two unique persons, initial experiences in **married love may be awkward and involve some experimentation**. Each person has rituals and preferences that make sexual love most satisfying. Couples should not worry about whether their practices are common or "normal," as long as they culminate in potentially procreative intercourse. Spouses should learn and honor each other's preferences and become increasingly aware of physical and emotional cues that indicate pleasure or discomfort. Couples must shape their mutual "sexual language" so that it promotes rather than inhibits wholeness and safety, dignifying and respecting the other instead of exalting selfish pleasure.

- *Self-stimulation or mutual stimulation* may assist but never replace intercourse. Habitual masturbation is a misuse of one's sexuality and may be a symptom of marital problems.

- *Pornography* introduces a third party into what should be an intimate sharing between two mutually exclusive partners. Pornography objectifies and degrades others for profit and is the antithesis of marital sexuality. Use of pornography supports an industry that enslaves human beings. Moreover, neuroscience has shown that its use may result in a compulsion that can rival addiction.

- *Role playing, fantasies, and sex aids* can never substitute for the partner or replace the partner's spontaneity and personality. While a playful attitude and certain outfits and goods can enhance marital sex, nothing should endanger, repulse, or injure either partner.

- *Open marriage*, or the introduction of any other person or persons into the sexual act, violates marital chastity. *Adultery* infringes on the wedding vows and effects a harmful separation of the spouses whether or not the other is aware of the infidelity.

- The use of *contraceptives* by prophylactic or medical means withholds one's fertility and whole self from one's spouse, which weakens the union. When contraceptive medication must be prescribed for other conditions, it may also result in temporary infertility.

- *Sterilization* is sometimes medically necessary or the unwanted secondary effect of another procedure. This is not morally problematic. Couples who must regulate the birth of their children should have honest conversations and arrive at an agreement. It is not appropriate for either partner to deliberately inhibit conception, and the desire to do so indicates problems.

- *Sexual addiction and illness* do exist, even in marriage. These include pornography use, pedophilia, the need to use prostitutes, chronic masturbation, and homosexual activity outside of marriage. Spouses who suspect having these inclinations have a moral obligation to reveal this to a priest or therapist, and eventually to share it with one's spouse. Such activity violates the marital commitment and carries the risk of sexually transmitted disease, blackmail, and physical harm. Sexual addictions are treatable but only with support and understanding.

- *Molestation and rape* are forced sexual acts that violate a person's right to give his or her body and sexuality to another by choice. God blesses each individual with free will, and even within the context of a committed, sacramental marriage, sexual acts are never guaranteed or owed. Acts of rape are horribly distorted and never contribute to happiness or unity.

What Is Marital Chastity?

Abstinence, virginity, celibacy, and chastity are related, but not the same. We might abstain from sex (or from any good thing) for a variety of reasons. Two valid reasons for sexual abstinence are to avoid out-of-wedlock pregnancy and sexually transmitted disease. Virginity and celibacy are permanent or long-term abstinence from sexual activity and may or may not have a spiritual motivation. For example, a person may never have had any genital experience, but not for lack of trying. Or an individual may avoid sex out of fear, anger, or bitterness. There is not much virtue in that.

Chastity is a virtue, a moral skill, that involves the proper and holy use of sexuality. Chastity may be celibate or virginal when it involves abstinence from sex for a higher reason, or it may be marital, in which "I engage in sexual activity only with my spouse, out of faith and with a desire to imitate Christ's love for his people."

Marital chastity is acquired over a lifetime. It starts at the first moments of attraction and evolves over time into a deep love born of commitment and self-giving. It is tempered by adversity, patience, and sacrifice. Marital chastity is a story of salvation that a couple begins to create when they pronounce their vows. They do not enter marriage as blank slates; each has a unique history and sexuality. This is why couples must cultivate a habit of honesty and transparency. They must acknowledge their hopes, anxieties, and past experiences if they are to build a common sexual language that admits of grace.

Sexual Wholeness

Sex engages our whole selves and all our senses. Below, jot down the "sensual" items that please you or that you are interested in experiencing in marriage.

Discuss your responses with your future spouse. What do you have in common? Does anything offend you or make you uncomfortable?

Eyes
Sight, such as staring deeply

Ears
Sound, such as love songs

Nose
Smell, such as roses

Mouth
Taste, such as kissing

Hands
Touch, such as caressing hair

137

For Reflection and Discussion

1. Try to recall when and how you learned about sex (in your family, school, media, and other avenues). Share one or two experiences and examples that explain your sexuality.

2. What do your experiences and history tell you about your attitudes and beliefs about sex? How are they are similar and different from those of your future spouse? In what ways do they reflect what you know about the Church's teaching on sexuality?

3. Do you think about sex as sacramental? Do you think sex can become part of your spiritual life? Are there ways besides sexual relations that your marriage can be generative, fruitful, and occasions of grace?

4. How do you feel about your own body? Think of an experience in which you became aware of your body reacting emotionally to something outside of yourself. What do you think that says about marital love and sexual attraction?

5. Is there anything about sex or sexuality that makes you afraid or anxious, especially as you prepare for marriage? What would it mean for your marriage if you experienced same-sex attraction?

My Thoughts

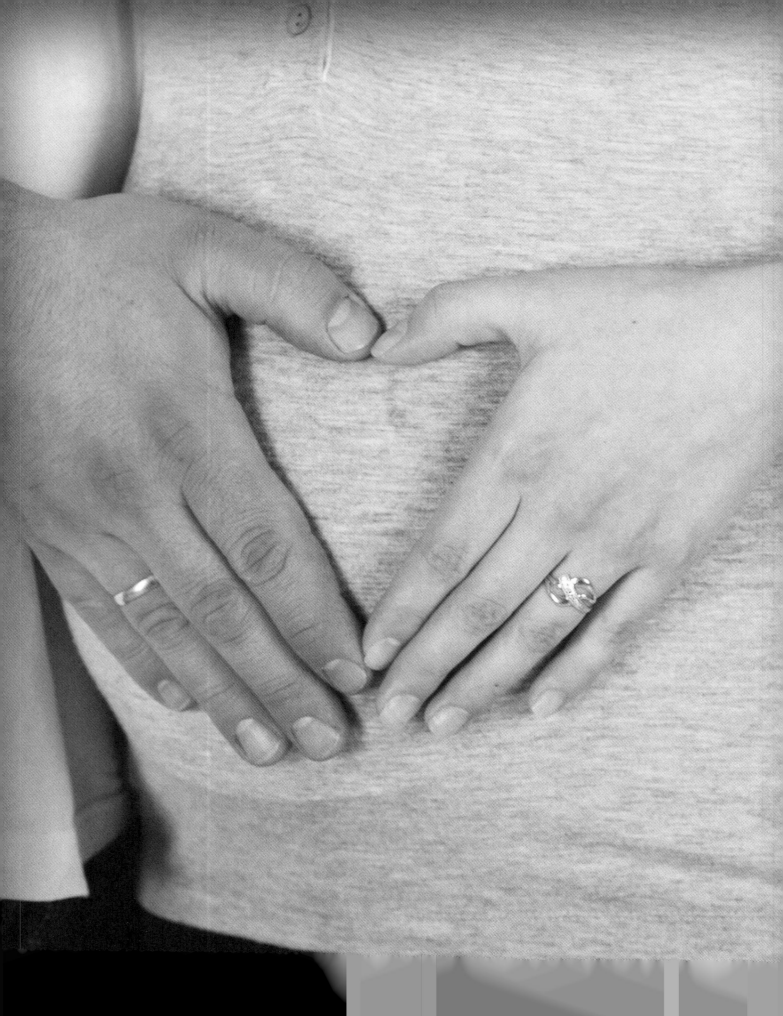

Natural Family Planning

Karen Jiménez Robles, MD

In this chapter...

- Approaching fertility and parenthood as a Christian couple
- Anatomy and the menstrual cycle
- Methods and advantages of NFP

Human fertility involves both a man and a woman and therefore must be dealt with as a couple. Both husband and wife must be taken into account in order to understand the greatness of procreation and the responsibility it implies.

Men and women should know and understand their bodies deeply in order to take care of them and use them properly. In the case of fertility, couples should seek to reach the point at which they can freely decide at any moment whether to welcome or postpone pregnancy.

Importantly: **Remember, parenthood is not a right.** Most people can have access with fairly high probability, but it doesn't always happen. The Church sees children as the "supreme gift of marriage," and while openness to life (procreation) is an essential aspect and duty of marriage, it is ordered toward the good of the spouses, of the children, and of the greater Church and society (*CCC* 2378; see also 2366–72).

Parenthood by adoption also is possible, but it is not a right, either. In adoption, parents are sought for a child, and not a child for parents. Adoption is real and true parenthood, although it is not based on a biological link. Both forms of parenthood show themselves in offering love and self-giving, which fulfills the goals of human sexuality.

This is the context in which natural family planning (NFP) belongs and thrives. **These methods use different signs to recognize the woman's fertile days** and offer couples a real alternative to altering their biological cycles. Strictly speaking, they are neither contraceptive nor "conceptive"; they give the couple better knowledge of the woman's fertility, which will help them to make better decisions about the family they wish to have.

Allow Jesus to use your fertility to further his divine plan.

Read about the parents below. How are the following practices expressed in the preparation for and reception of a child?

Parent(s)	Child	Verses	Practice(s)	Response
Abraham and Sarah	Isaac	Genesis 18:1–15; 21:1–8	Hospitality	
Elkanah and Hannah	Samuel	1 Samuel 1	Prayer	
Zechariah and Elizabeth	John the Baptist	Luke 1:5–25, 57–80	Service & Sacrifice	
Mary	Jesus	Luke 1:26–56; 2:1–21	Proclamation & Evangelization	

How can you foster these traits in your marriage both before and after having children? Approaching conception and childbirth with faith and hope will strengthen your marriage and add meaning to parenthood.

Anatomy and Physiology

The human male, unless inhibited by illness, is always fertile. **His fertility begins at puberty and continues throughout his life.** With age, his procreative capacity diminishes somewhat, but he continues to be considered fertile because his testicles continue to produce spermatozoa.

The lifespan of the sperm depends on the presence or absence of cervical mucus, which the woman produces in her fertile period. In the presence of this mucus, a **sperm can live from three to five days inside the vagina;** without this mucus it lives for a few hours or even just a few minutes.

Unlike the male, the human female is mostly infertile. A healthy woman's fertility depends on the functioning of the ovary and is limited to a determined time. She is fertile starting at her first menstruation, called menarche, until the last one, menopause. **Within the monthly cycle, the woman's body favors conception for only eight to eleven days.** During the other days, pregnancy is impossible.

The ovum, once expelled, lives between twelve and twenty-four hours.

This information helps us correct false perceptions about how easy or common conception is. We often hear about unexpected pregnancies, but the fact is, people don't usually talk about infertile intercourse, because it is rarely relevant. Intercourse that leads to pregnancy, though much less frequent, has higher visibility and greater impact to the family and society at large.

Contraceptive methods have also contributed to the false perception that pregnancy is the most frequent result of the conjugal act. Within a woman's fertile phase, the rate of fertility is 20 percent. That is to say, **of every five couples who have sex during the fertile period, only one will achieve pregnancy**. This conclusion is from a strictly statistical point of view.

The Menstrual Cycle

To achieve or postpone pregnancy intentionally, a woman must know her menstrual cycle. Most important is to recognize the moment when ovulation occurs so the woman can pinpoint easily when she is fertile.

The menstrual cycle has four phases:

1. Menstruation
2. Preovulatory infertile phase
3. Fertile phase (ovulation)
4. Postovulatory infertile phase

There are also three kinds of cycles, distinguished by their length:

1. Short cycle: <24 days
2. Regular cycle: 25–38 days
3. Long cycle: 38+ days

In order to calculate the length of a menstrual cycle, the **first day of menstrual bleeding is day one,** and the last day is the day immediately preceding the next menstrual bleeding. From a biological standpoint, we could say that a cycle begins with ovulation, or even with the maturation of the follicles, and ends with menstruation, a process through which the unfertilized ovum disintegrates and is discarded. But we call the former the "menstrual cycle" because menstruation is the clearest sign that allows a woman to better orient herself to the functioning of her body.

Menstruation

Menstruation is the easiest phase to recognize, although the way each woman's body behaves during those days may vary. **Bleeding normally lasts from three to eight days.** During menstruation, the woman's body discards both the unfertilized ovum and the material that it had prepared in order to receive the embryo in case fertilization occurred. For that to happen, the cervix has to open. As it happens, when the cervix opens, the spermatozoa can also pass through and reach the uterus and, eventually, the Fallopian tubes.

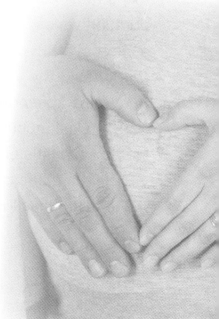

This phase is considered fertile because some women—typically those with short cycles—begin their fertile period before or on the last day of bleeding or spotting. Therefore, **the last days of menstruation are considered fertile** because sperm can live up to five days in the presence of cervical mucus, which appears before and during ovulation.

This is one of the practical difficulties of this period. During this phase, the woman feels wet on the outside of her genital region, but due to menstrual bleeding, it is not easy to distinguish whether cervical mucus is present.

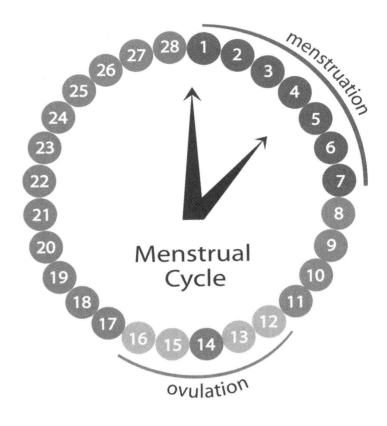

Menstrual Cycle

menstruation

ovulation

Pre-ovulatory infertile phase

This phase lasts from the end of menstruation until fertile signs appear. Its duration varies, and in some women with a short cycle, it may be nonexistent. **In this phase, the woman often feels "dry"** due to the absence of vaginal secretions. Any cervical mucus present at this point would have little elasticity.

There are basically two factors that make this phase infertile. The first is that the cervix closes when the bleeding has ended because the female's immune system produces a barrier of thick mucus to impede the entrance of any microorganism into the uterus, avoiding infections. With the cervix closed and protected in this way, sperm cannot enter. The second factor is that the vaginal walls become more acidic during this period, which impedes infections and also creates a hostile environment for sperm.

Fertile phase

The fertile phase begins on the first day the woman produces cervical mucus, that is, when she feels that zone of her body to be moist or slippery. Cervical mucus is a sign that the pituitary follicle-stimulating hormone, also known as FSH, is present and starting to recruit ovarian follicles, the cells that store the ovum as they mature. When a follicle bursts, one of the ova is expelled from the ovary. This is the process of ovulation. This happens once every cycle.

While the follicles grow and mature, the hormone estradiol is secreted, signaling the cervix to dilate and produce more elastic cervical mucus. **As the days pass, the mucus changes its color and consistency.** Estradiol also signals the endometrium, the tissue lining the inside of the uterus, to grow, allowing the embryo to implant itself and be nurtured until the placenta is formed.

During this phase, the cervical mucus nourishes, transports, supports, and filters the semen so that only the best sperm have access to the uterus. Without this mucus it is practically impossible for the sperm to reach the Fallopian tubes. Many women are not familiar with this type of secretion. **It often brings a slippery sensation to that zone of their body.** This is similar to, but separate from, arousal fluid, which can be thinner and disappear shortly after stimulation.

The disappearance of the mucus is a sign that ovulation has taken place. The expelled ovum then has twenty-four hours to be fertilized. In other words, if the intention of the couple is to postpone pregnancy, they should mark when the mucus with the most fertile characteristics has completely disappeared, count three days (to be sure the fertile period is over), and only then resume intercourse as desired.

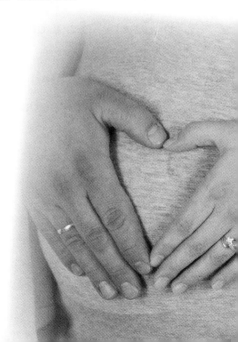

Postovulatory infertile phase

This phase lasts from one day after ovulation until menstruation. This is the most stable phase of the cycle, and it consistently lasts from nine to seventeen days. That is to say, the **duration varies from woman to woman, but it typically lasts the same amount of time in each woman.**

Once the ovum is expelled, it may encounter sperm in the Fallopian tube and be fertilized. From there it travels to the uterus for implantation. During that time, progesterone prepares the uterus to receive the embryo by supporting the development of the endometrium. It also provokes an increase of basal body temperature, the temperature of the body when waking up after having slept more than five hours. (It can be measured in the mouth, armpit, or vagina.) Therefore, **body temperature can also be used as a sign of when ovulation has taken place.**

One day after ovulation, the cervix closes and again produces a mucus barrier. If conception has not occurred, the woman returns to an infertile period. This phase ends with menstruation, the start of a new cycle.

Getting to Know You

Select the best response to these questions, given your current knowledge and beliefs. Then share and discuss your responses with your future spouse. Use this time to correct assumptions and develop a shared approach to your fertility.

1. I consider my anatomy and fertility to be...

Him	Her	
☐	☐	Advanced / Abundant
☐	☐	Normal / Healthy
☐	☐	Limited / Challenged
☐	☐	Sterile / Impotent

2. If we experienced a pregnancy, it would be...

Him	Her	
☐	☐	Disappointing
☐	☐	Disastrous
☐	☐	Exciting
☐	☐	Miraculous
☐	☐	Wonderful
☐	☐	I'm not sure

3. We would like to have ... children.

Him	Her	
☐	☐	0
☐	☐	1–2
☐	☐	3–4
☐	☐	5–6
☐	☐	7+

4. We would like our first child to be...

Him	Her	
☐	☐	A Girl
☐	☐	A Boy
☐	☐	Twins / Multiples
☐	☐	Whatever God chooses

5. Our openness to adoption is...

Him	Her	
☐	☐	None
☐	☐	Slight
☐	☐	Moderate
☐	☐	Strong
☐	☐	Undecided
☐	☐	We intend to adopt (or have already).

6. Our openness to practicing NFP in marriage is...

Him	Her	
☐	☐	None
☐	☐	Slight
☐	☐	Moderate
☐	☐	Strong
☐	☐	Undecided
☐	☐	We/She already use(s) a method of NFP.

History and Methods of Family Planning

Fertility studies have helped to develop numerous methods that help couples decide when to have a baby. Known as "family planning methods," they are classified as natural or artificial.

Natural methods **seek to identify a woman's fertile and infertile days without altering the functioning of her body** or the sexual act. They offer spouses the possibility of deciding if they want to have a pregnancy or not. As they respect the natural cycle, there are no medical contraindications or side effects.

Artificial methods are medicines or devices that intervene in the natural mechanisms of fertility, modifying the organism or the way in which the sexual act is realized. *They are not suitable for everyone* and can present serious side effects.

Many consider artificial methods to be the most reliable, efficacious, and convenient. Natural methods are considered less dependable and more complicated. This is untrue. **Many simple, safe, natural methods are as effective, if not more so, than artificial methods** at postponing or achieving pregnancy.

Furthermore, due to the attentive observation of the female's reproductive functioning, natural methods can quickly and more easily detect risks to the woman's health, such as a physical anomaly or gynecological condition. Because they are medically safe, **they can be used diagnostically regardless of sexual activity** and during puberty, breastfeeding, and premenopause.

Advantages of Natural Family Planning

- Instead of introducing devices or substances into the woman's body, NFP offers *information* about the body's functioning so a woman can know if she is fertile or not at any given moment.

- The information gathered in the practice of NFP can be, and has been, used to diagnose and treat a number of gynecological and reproductive disorders and diseases.

- NFP is medically safe. It does not produce any side effects or alter or compromise the health of the woman, sexual partner, or any developing baby.

- NFP encourages the couple to be involved in the practice and implementation of the method, aiding communication and shared decision-making.

- NFP approaches sexuality in the context of an interpersonal relationship of respect and concern, as well as responsible parenthood. When used in conjunction with temporary abstinence, the couple's relationship and the sexual act itself take on greater relevance and return to the spiritual plane. Sex continues to occupy a central place in the life of the couple, but it is not given exaggerated importance, which can paradoxically depersonalize it.

- NFP is adaptable to the specific needs of each woman or couple. In most cases, NFP can be used at any age or in any reproductive stage: puberty, pregnancy, breastfeeding, menopause, etc.

Natural Family Planning Methods

CRITERIA	METHOD NAME	CREATED	FORM OF USE
Probabilistic calculation of fertile days	OGINO-KNAUS (rhythm or calendar method)	1924-1928	Predicts fertile days based on the duration of the last 12 cycles; the resulting days are cataloged as the fertile days of each cycle.
	STANDARD DAYS METHOD	Georgetown University	Women count their cycles on a loop of beads numbered and colored to predict fertile and infertile days.
Observation of cervical mucus	BILLINGS OVULATION METHOD ™	1953 Australia	Based on making regular observations of the cervical mucus to define each day as fertile or infertile
	CREIGHTON MODEL FertilityCare™ SYSTEM	1976 USA	Based on the standardized observing and recording of biological markers, indicating the fertile days during each cycle
Observation of basal body temperature	BABY-COMP® LADY-COMP® PEARLY®	1987 Germany	Electronic devices developed to measure and record changes in basal body temperature
Interpretation of various signs of fertility	Sympto-Thermal	1980	Combines the interpretation of basal temperature, cervical mucus, mood, etc., and daily recording to identify fertile days precisely
	Marquette Method Sympto-hormonal	1999	Uses electronic monitor to detect the levels of hormones in urine; combines the interpretation of multiple signs to identify fertile days precisely
Determination of hormone levels in urine (estradiol, LH)	Persona®	1996 England	Uses disposable sticks to detect hormone levels in urine; measurements are taken on different days of the cycle to better predict ovulation
	Clearblue®	1985 USA	Uses disposable sticks to detect hormone levels in urine and detect the woman's most fertile days
Determination of electrolyte levels	Ovacue®	1970 USA	A monitor that measures levels of electrolytes in saliva to determine fertility

EFFECTIVENESS FOR SPACING PREGNANCY	EFFECTIVENESS IN SEEKING PREGNANCY	COMMENTS
90–70%	—	Only useful for women with regular cycles of 26–32 days.
95% (correct use) 88% (typical use)[1]	—	
95%	78%	Simple and easy to learn. It may be used during breastfeeding.
97%–83%[2, 3]	98–76%	Also detects any alterations in gyneco-logical and reproductive health. It may be used during breastfeeding.
98%[4, 5, 6]	—	
99.8%–94%	—	
99% (perfect use) 86%–93% [7, 8]	85%	May be used during breastfeeding
94% [9, 10]	—	Only useful for women with regular cycles of 23–35 days
99.4% [11, 12]	—	Only marketed for achieving and not avoiding pregnancy
98% [13]	—	Can be used during breastfeeding

1. standarddaysmethod.org

2. creightonmodel.com/effectiveness.htm

3. Stanford, Joseph B., MD, MSPH. *Effectiveness, Intention, and Behavior: Creighton Model NFP Use.* Salt Lake City: University of Utah. January 2009. ent-s-t.com/OFP_Natural/documents/University%20of%20Utah.pdf

4. Freundl G, Godehardt E, Kern PA, Frank-Herrmann P, Koubenec HJ, Gnoth C. Estimated maximum failure rates of cycle monitors using daily conception probabilities in the menstrual cycle. *Human Reproduction.* 2003; 18(12): 2628–33.

5. Frank-Herrmann P, Heil J, Gnoth C, et al. The effectiveness of a fertility awareness based method to avoid pregnancy in relation to a couple's sexual behavior during the fertile time: a prospective longitudinal study. *Human Reprod.* 2007; 22(5): 1310–9.

6. De Leizaola MA. Etude prospective d'efficacité d'une méthode sympto-thermique récente de planning familial natural. *J Gynecol Obstet Biol Reprod.* 1998; 27: 174–80.

7. Fehring RJ, Schneider M, Lee Barron M. Efficacy of the Marquette Method of natural family planning. *Am J Matern Child Nurs.* 2008; 33(6): 348–54.

8. nfp.marquette.edu/efficacy.php

9. persona.info/uk/what_is.php

10. Janssen CJ, van Lunsen RH. Profile and opinions of the female Persona user in The Netherlands. *Eur J Contracept Reprod Health Care.* 2000; 5(2): 141–6.

11. Guida M, Bramante S, Acunzo G, Pellicano M, Cirillo D, Nappi C. Diagnosis of fertility with a personal hormonal evaluation test. *Minerva Ginecol.* 2003; 55(2): 167–73.

12. clearblueeasy.com/clearblue-easy-fertility-monitor-faq.php

13. ovacue.com/ovacue-vs-other-methods-ovulation-prediction

The NFP Lifestyle

The *Creighton Model Fertility Care System* seeks to strengthen marital intimacy and interaction through five pillars summarized in the acronym SPICE (below). The more these areas are strengthened in a marriage, the more profound the sexuality, with less risk of reducing it to mere genital contact. Many other methods offer similar support. NFP offers a couple spiritual and moral underpinnings.

Spiritual
How is your faith shared, intimate, even transcendent? Give an example.

Physical
How do you express affection and closeness without genital contact?

Intellectual
What learning and/or projects do you attain together? (These sessions count!)

Creative/Communicative
What have you created (or will you create) together other than offspring? What written or verbal forms of communication do you use?

Emotional
Do you share dreams, desires, even humor as well as your bodies? How does a healthy sexuality care for emotional feelings as much as physical sensations?

NFP Training

1. Select one method of NFP you'd like to try as a couple, and research available instructors and providers in your area. The chart in this chapter and your leaders are a good start.

2. Schedule an introductory or training session and attend it together. Couples who enter marriage with a shared understanding of their fertility and reproductive goals are gifted with a level of comfort, unity, and purpose.

3. Allow yourselves to gain some confidence with your chosen method free from the pressures of conception. You should be able to freely offer information and reactions to your shared fertility as you enter marital relations.

For Reflection and Discussion

1. What are the differences between male and female fertility? Review with each other the four phases of a woman's cycle.

2. What is the probability of becoming pregnant in each conjugal act during a woman's fertile phase?

3. What advantages do natural methods offer over artificial contraception? Do the natural methods seem reliable to you? Why or why not?

4. What characteristics would you look for in a family planning method?

5. What is involved in responsible parenthood?

My Thoughts

_____
_____
_____
_____
_____
_____
_____
_____
_____
_____
_____
_____
_____
_____
_____
_____
_____
_____
_____

Children and Parenting

Coleen Kelly Mast

In this chapter…

- Children are gifts to their parents and society.
- Parenting styles may vary based on gender or personality.
- Families bond by working, playing, and praying together.

In man and woman's giving of themselves to one another, new life results. Their love and union naturally beget human life. **Marriage itself, and in particular the conjugal act of marriage, is ordained toward procreation and parenthood**. Co-creating with God, especially in the conception of a child, is a mystery and a miracle. Pregnancy and parenting can be a deeply joyful experience. They bring new levels of fulfillment to a husband and wife's marital bond and life together.

In the Order of Celebrating Matrimony, the couple affirms their call and agrees to "accept children lovingly from God." God is the inexhaustible source of that love, which sustains the spouses and their children. God gives you children to love and to nurture so their souls bring joy to the world and all may live in eternal joy. **Each child—biological, adopted, or otherwise accepted—is full of God-given qualities.** Each new child touches your heart and can increase your capacity to love.

Children Are a Gift to Marriage

"Be fruitful and multiply, and fill the earth and subdue it" (Genesis 1:28).

"Children are really the supreme gift to marriage and contribute very substantially to the welfare of their parents" (*Gaudium et Spes,* 50).

How can parenting be a gift?

1. ***When spouses become parents, their love is multiplied.*** The joy and amazement of pregnancy are natural and healthy, since the fetus points to the mysteries of conception, creation, and mutual love. The witness of your love and children displays God's authentic and natural vision of love, life, sexuality, and marriage throughout the family and society. Everyone is richer when Christian families grow.

2. ***Love for your child(ren) is a unifying force.*** Sharing in the love and care of a child who looks like both of you, whom you created together with God, joins you emotionally and socially and keeps you from growing apart or going your own separate or selfish ways.

3. ***Your child(ren) call forth the best in you.*** Rising to the occasion of parenting helps you to mature and lead your family by example. Each child will bring unique challenges; some will try your patience, others will question your need for peace and quiet. When your hearts warm to the needs of a helpless person, you become more self-giving. When you see your spouse respond selflessly to your child, you may be inspired by the goodness you see.

Baby Pictures

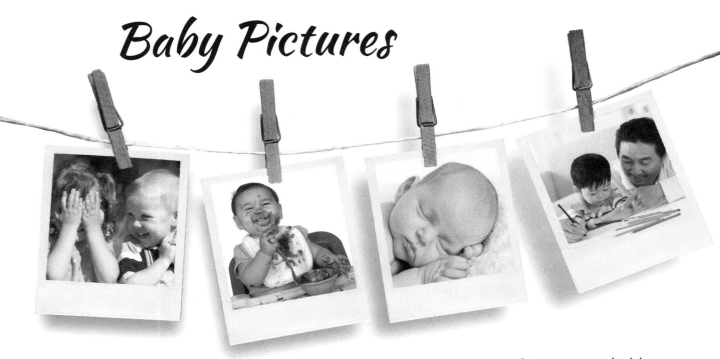

1. Circle the phrases that you identify as "cute" or that create a positive reaction in yourself. How does your ideal image of children and parenting differ from your future spouse's?

   - A smiling baby
   - A sleeping baby
   - A naked / bathing baby
   - A cooing / babbling baby
   - A messy baby (food, dirt)
   - Children walking / climbing
   - Children talking
   - Children playing
   - Children praying / praising
   - Children performing / excelling
   - Parents admiring / touching a pregnant belly
   - Parents holding / hugging
   - Parents reading / singing
   - Parents teaching / sharing
   - Parents playing / befriending

2. When you think of pregnancy, babies, children, or parenting, what images or memories come to mind?

   _____

   _____

   _____

   _____

   _____

   _____

   _____

   _____

Children Change the Marriage

As couples approach marriage, they often dream of having children. Some might plan out an "ideal" number of children, and others may just "see how it goes." Some couples may already have children, separately or together; others may never be able to conceive. Some couples choose to adopt, whether or not they have biological children. Couples of faith often find that trusting in God's grace and being open to new life can bring greater rewards than planning everything out for themselves. **God calls all couples to be responsible and not careless, to use the natural methods of fertility awareness, and to make their decisions with prayerful consideration and a generous spirit.** Recalling that there are three people in a marriage— the husband, the wife, and God—it is good to consult all three, especially the wisest one.

The practical realities of parenting often come before the baby is born, perhaps in the form of morning sickness, furnishing the nursery, or preparing

other household members. After baby arrives, time together may have to be planned; changes in sleep may affect moods; and the budget may need to be adjusted. However, all can be endured and even enjoyed just as generations before you have—in faith and love, with God's grace, and by the support of the entire Christian community.

God provides some additional help through hormones (such as oxytocin or prolactin) that assist both mothers and fathers to become more compassionate—even toward that child who stays up all night with a fever or needs to nurse more often. More than one parent has taken that late-night time for prayer and thanksgiving. As the years pass, don't lose the real meaning of life and love or the wonder and awe of God's gifts. What your child needs most is your love and nurturing, which cannot be bought or delegated.

As your family grows, so will your challenges and strengths. God continually offers you the graces through the sacrament as you continue to say, "I do" daily. You may find that those vows—for better or for worse, for richer or poorer, in sickness and in health—were not empty words. **You will experience the ups and downs of life as a family, but the more generous you are, the more strength and wisdom you will receive.** Some of a family's dearest memories are made while going through difficult times.

Parents lead their children to God.

PSALM 34:12

"Come, children, listen to me; I will teach you fear of the Lord."

Name three things you want your children to know about God.

1. _____
2. _____
3. _____

MATTHEW 5:9

"Blessed are the peacemakers, for they will be called children of God."

Name three ways you can cultivate peace within your home and family.

1. _____
2. _____
3. _____

ZECHARIAH 10:7

"Their children will see and rejoice—their hearts will exult in the LORD."

Name three moments, events, or ways you can celebrate or worship as a Christian family.

1. _____
2. _____
3. _____

EPHESIANS 6:1, 4

"Children, obey your parents [in the Lord], for this is right... Fathers, do not provoke your children to anger, but bring them up with the training and instruction of the Lord."

Name three behaviors or rules that model Christian living for all family members.

1. _____
2. _____
3. _____

Gender Differences and Parenting Styles

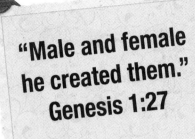

"Male and female he created them."
Genesis 1:27

God created two sexes, equal in dignity, different in many physical and psychological ways, yet made to complement each other. **Having two parents, one male and one female, was God's idea, programmed directly within our bodies**. Behind the science of conception, pregnancy, and breastfeeding are many deeply embedded meanings about mothering and fathering that we may never fully comprehend. This scientific reality of parenting is God's brilliant design and thus benefits the development of the child he creates through their love.

This gender complementarity offers a balanced and comprehensive set of gifts, one that children recognize from the beginning. Fetuses respond to the familiar sounds of the mother's heartbeat and voice. Newborns turn to the smell of Mom's milk, and her body reacts by producing nourishment. Dad may hum, hold, or rock the baby perfectly to sleep. But besides the physical roles, our personalities may complement one another, too. When one parent is stressed or exhausted, the other can step in. Where one is more empathetic, the other might be more logical. One may be stricter while the other is more lenient. A husband and wife should be each other's helpmates by encouraging and caring for one another, trusting that together with God, you will become excellent parents.

Parenting styles are not only influenced by gender but also by temperament, communication style, and the discipline style of your family of origin. Some differences are hormonal and psychological; others may have been learned.

166

Parenting may come naturally to some, but it also takes practice. You may wish to take classes on parenting or discipline together. In any case, God will help you develop the knowledge, instincts, and abilities you need to fulfill your vocation. You can build consistency and nurturing as you cooperatively guide your children. When parents strive to be on the same page, work together in love, and don't undermine each other, they can both offer their unique gifts to their children, assisting each one to become the young man or woman that God wants them to be.

What Would You Do?

Discuss the following parenting scenarios and describe an effective response that reflects understanding, compassion, and reconciliation.

1. Brayden is three years old. While you are preparing his meal, he begins to reach above the table. You move the sharp and fragile items away and ask him to wait patiently. He only whines more.

2. Paul is ten years old. One of his regular chores is to rake the yard. One week, a large school project keeps him busy, and he neglects this task. Acknowledging the situation, he requests permission to attend a friend's party.

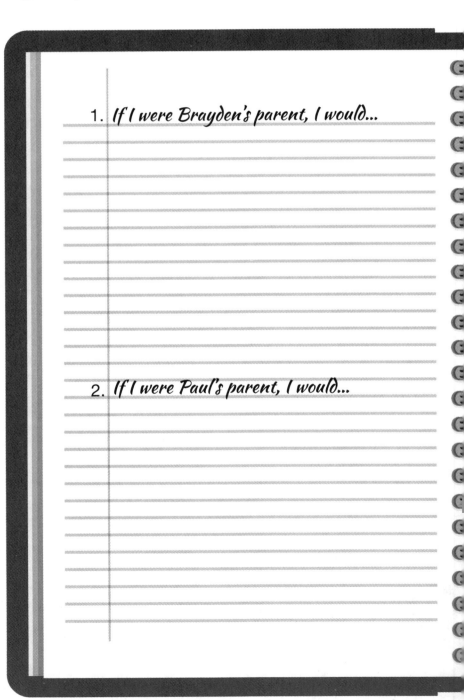

1. *If I were Brayden's parent, I would...*

2. *If I were Paul's parent, I would...*

3. *If I were Veronica's parent, I would...*

3. Veronica is nineteen and living at home while attending college. Her boyfriend and she return home later and later, then occasionally the next morning. When questioned, she denies any wrongdoing and claims you are invading her privacy.

4. *If I were their parent, I would...*

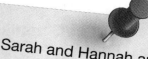

4. Sarah and Hannah are eight-year-old twins. One of their shared and favorite activities is dancing. This year, their annual recital is scheduled on a Saturday night. You have another family obligation the next morning and planned to attend the vigil Mass to avoid a too-early service.

Family Bonding: Building the Domestic Church

The Christian family constitutes a specific revelation and realization of ecclesial communion, and for this reason too it can and should be called "the domestic Church."

Pope St. John Paul II, *Familiaris Consortio* 21, see CCC 2204

God is a communion of persons—Father, Son, and Holy Spirit. The Church, and parents in particular, are called to model this deep unity. Through baptism, new disciples are born; through the witness and example of parents in the family, children learn to live as members of the Church.

Parents are called to create an atmosphere of Christian joy in their homes. Adapting Gospel values, the family is made to nurture, instruct, and affirm the good in each family member. This can be difficult when life is busy or demanding, or in periods of great suffering—all times when we must turn to God in prayer.

The family becomes your place of prayer, peace, and respite—like an oasis from worldly concerns. Disagreements or arguments should always work toward positive resolutions, not food for wounded egos. Rooted in love, a family should make a concerted effort to *work together, play together, and pray together*.

Work Together

Teamwork is essential to a strong and intimate family. This begins with the parents working as a team on various projects and extends as the children grow. Although teamwork includes a fair division of household duties, it means much more than "who does what." **Just as a sports team requires players to practice some skills on their own, the team comes together to reach the goal**. Spending time together while everyone does his or her part creates a sense of unity and satisfaction worth celebrating at the end.

Working together as a team can include planning vacations, setting up a business, home projects, and even apostolic works that serve the needy. For example, teamwork for daily meals includes each person's share in the planning, shopping, preparing, setting, serving, or cleaning up of a meal. Each person can make a contribution and experience the fulfillment of participation. Working together helps combat individualism and selfishness.

Working together is a necessary skill and invaluable for growing in virtue. For example, we practice patience when we teach a child how to do something we already know well. We learn how to respect each other's time and to persevere by being prompt and diligent, avoiding the natural tendency to laziness. When one person wants to do the job quickly and another wants to do it meticulously, how can we use both qualities to do the job well?

Like all of God's gifts, children help us grow in holiness and get to heaven. **As your child grows, you will see yourself alive, as you really are—** reflected back in language and intonations, in attitudes and principles.

This helps us better examine our words and behavior and ask ourselves, "What good habits should I develop, knowing that these habits will be duplicated by my children and spread to the world?" When necessary, correct one another with love. The home is not the place to magnify each other's weaknesses but to lovingly help each other to overcome their faults. It is good to develop the habits of:

- Many more affirmations than criticism
- Much more forgiveness than blaming
- Much more compassion than anger
- Much more fun than tension (but never joking at the expense of another's feelings)

Play Together

Family "down time," just as with "quality time" with our spouse and children, must often be scheduled and planned. Relaxation is necessary to human health and well-being, and togetherness helps create family bonds that can withstand the storms of life. If you do not take the time to build a strong family, it will not just happen on its own.

Set priorities and limits as a family, and take advantage of these opportunities:

- Family meals as a means to unity. Strive for at least one every day.

- Peaceful bedtimes for both children and parents.

- Family fun times that break up the stress of the day, week, or month.

- Sunday and holy-day Sabbaths that include Mass, relaxation, and time with God and nature. (Even God rested on the seventh day.)

- Regular dates for mom and dad to strengthen their bond and have fun.

- Family vacations—besides those extended family visits—to seal the nuclear-family bond.

Pray Together

In order to lead our children to heaven, we must pray with them and live a life of virtue. The good example of parents begins with taking the children to weekly Mass, praying together as a family, and keeping the Ten Commandments. Bless each member of your family each morning and offer your day to God. Bless them again each night before bed. Pray and bless your meals and snacks. Parents should strive to become the best they can be before God, to grow in love and grace, embracing the virtues of faith, hope, love, prudence, justice, fortitude, and temperance.

Family Life Chart

In a few words, fill in each box with your ideas on each topic. An example is provided.

	His ideas			Her ideas		
	Who	**What**	**When**	**Who**	**What**	**When**
Vacations	He & the guys	Camping	Hunting season	Husband & wife	Resort on beach	A winter reprieve
Family downtime	Parents & kids together	Watching television	After dinner	Each member individually	Reading books	After dinner

	My ideas		
	Who	**What**	**When**
Chores			
Household projects			
Family downtime			
Vacations			
Parenting			
Raising and educating kids			

Review each other's responses and start a conversation on your married family life.

Where do your differences create balance? Where is further unity needed?

(In the example, the couple has some discussing and compromising to do.)

For Reflection and Discussion

1. What were the strengths of your parent(s) and your upbringing? What were the weaknesses? What do you treasure most about your future spouse and your relationship?

2. Discuss how your marriage might change as you have children. Share your thoughts and feelings on having one parent stay home or put her or his career on hold to care for the children. Will (or how will) you live on one income?

3. Reflect on the responsibility you will have for your child(ren)'s spiritual welfare. Discuss what this means to each of you and the ways you plan to foster their relationship with God. Share some early experiences with prayer, faith, religion, and the sacraments.

4. Do you currently watch, care for, or interact with children? What do you think your parenting style will be? Describe your ideal or perfect mother and father.

5. Share examples of how you were disciplined as a child. Discuss what you believe about child discipline and punishment.

My Thoughts

_____
_____
_____
_____
_____
_____
_____
_____
_____
_____
_____
_____
_____
_____
_____
_____
_____
_____
_____

Cohabitation

Cassandra L. Hough

In this chapter...

- The truth about marriage, sex, and Catholic teaching
- Debunking the myths of cohabitation and compatibility
- Transitioning to marriage and chastity

For Christine and her husband, the first year of marriage was filled with disagreements about how to live together. Having lived separately before getting married, they felt they had missed out on the domestic "practice run" that other couples seem to get by cohabiting. Perhaps, prior to their wedding day, they had ignored each other's household practices (unfolded clothes, piles of books, and bills), but once they were under a single roof, these habits became the source of everyday annoyances.

Is the wait to live together worth it? Although faith is an important reason for living separately before marriage, **couples admit that they want their married life to feel new and different** from their prior experiences. Like Christine and her husband, couples who lived apart until after the wedding discover that the lifelong commitment of the covenant greatly influences how they respond to one another's habits and work through disagreements. Cohabiting couples often question their compatibility, frequently weighing whether they can live with their partner's quirks. Couples who wait to share their domestic lives approach their "incompatibilities" with a pro-relational attitude of finding a system to make living together work for both of them—for a lifetime.

The benefits of living separately before marriage receive little attention or acknowledgment. With cohabitation preceding more than 60 percent of first marriages, compared to almost none a half-century ago*, it is no wonder it is taken as the norm in American culture. Social scientists debate its benefits and risks; pastoral leaders discuss its effect on marriage preparation; and couples face questions about its timing, role, and meaning for their relationship.

*The National Marriage Project and the Institute for American Values, *The State of Our Unions: Marriage in America 2012* (Charlottesville: The National Marriage Project and the Institute for American Values, 2012), 76

Getting Church Teaching Straight

In his apostolic exhortation *Familiaris Consortio*, Pope St. John Paul II writes, "The Church must therefore promote better and more intensive programs of marriage preparation, in order to eliminate as far as possible the difficulties that many married couples find themselves in, and even more in order to favor positively the establishing and maturing of successful marriages" (66). It is in this light that we aim to help couples reflect on the decisions, behaviors, and qualities that best dispose them for a happy marriage. It is important to be clear: *Living together does not itself prohibit a couple from getting married in the Catholic Church*. Title VII of the *Code of Canon Law* (1083–1094) lists those qualities that are considered impediments to a valid marriage, such as impotence, sacred orders, a public perpetual vow of chastity, consanguinity, and being bound by a previous marriage.

However, **while cohabitation does not invalidate or prevent marriage, the Church strongly advises against it**.

Why?

Cohabitation is understood to consist not only of shared living quarters but also of sexual intimacy and intercourse prior to marriage. Although premarital sex, like cohabitation, does not itself impede a marriage, the Church is very clear about the significant meaning and purpose of sex and its proper place within marriage. Sexual intercourse and the intimate behaviors that attend it are reserved for marriage precisely because they give unique and fitting physical expression to the intimate, self-giving, and unitive nature of the marital relationship. **Sex expresses and makes physically present the two-become-one union of marriage.**

To express such unity where it does not exist—in other words, to have sex outside of marriage—is a serious affront to and abuse of the beauty of sex, the significance of marriage, and the dignity of men and women. Saint John Paul II touches upon this in *Familiaris Consortio* when he writes that experimenting through a "trial marriage" (cohabitation) is inconsistent with the dignity of the human person and the type of love this dignity demands (80). Therefore, the Church must advise against cohabitation and encourage all sexually active couples to take advantage of the sacrament of penance to make up for any offenses in this area and to receive the graces needed to live out God's truth about love and intimacy.

In addition to the moral and spiritual concerns, the Church has some very practical concerns about cohabitation. The *Catechism* states that, unlike true marriage, cohabiting cannot "ensure mutual sincerity and fidelity" nor protect against "inconstancy of desires or whim." Simply put, "human love does not tolerate 'trial marriages'" (*CCC* 2391).

In other words, people cannot simply "try on" marriage for a time. **There is no way to "try on" the complete and lifelong fidelity and commitment** that are inherent and essential to a true and sacramental marriage—whether through cohabitation, premarital relations, or any other means.

True Love

Sometimes partners will make demands by saying, "If you loved me, you would…."
While love and intimacy are self-giving, they are never possessive, conditional,
diminish one's identity, or compromise values and the truth.

How can the following express real, Christian love?
How can they distort or feign true love?

"Loving" Act	Is Real When…	Is Fake When…
Paying for meals or bills / Giving gifts		
Sharing pet- or child-care duties		
Staying late or overnight		
Spending time with an adult of the opposite sex		
Engaging in sexual activity with less than full interest or desire		

Debunking the Myths

Do the Church's concerns have any bearing on whether or not cohabitation is actually harmful to couples? Shouldn't individual couples be able to assess whether cohabitation is a good idea for them? Each couple has its own story and reasons for cohabiting. As unique as these may be, most rationales for living together tend to be based on at least one of three major assumptions:

1. Cohabitation is more convenient than living separately.
2. Cohabitation helps test compatibility.
3. Cohabitation ensures against future divorce.

Let's examine these assumptions and whether human experience reveals them to live up to their promises or not.

Cohabitation is more convenient than living separately.

For many couples, the transition to living together seems to just happen on its own. The couple will spend nights together multiple times a week, and one person's things gradually find residence at the other person's home. The inconvenience and expense of living separately often prompt couples to perceive moving in together as the better option.

As natural and clear as this transition may appear, it is frequently associated with a great deal of ambiguity surrounding each partner's intentions for cohabiting and underlying understanding of what cohabiting means for the progression of their relationship and their respective levels of commitment. This ambiguity becomes problematic when we consider the constraints that living together puts on a relationship.

The sharing of obligations and possessions—a lease, furniture, pets, perhaps even a child—naturally make it more difficult to break up. Even though couples may think they can easily end the relationship at any time, **the resulting momentum may cause couples to favor staying together despite finding themselves incompatible** and to drift into marriage without a clear, deliberative, mutual understanding of their commitment to each other and whether or not they are truly well-suited to be together.

Additionally, the idea that cohabiting is more convenient financially is misleading. While cohabiting couples may seek out the freedom of shared living expenses, cohabiting often does not result in improved savings. Financial savings are not solely dependent on the pooled resources and energies of the couple. How the couple decides to spend or invest their money is also a key factor, along with the level to which they pool their income. It is here that **the degree of permanence and mutual dependence in the relationship makes a difference**. Cohabiting couples actually combine their resources less than those who are married. As a result, their reported wealth is similar to that of single people and significantly below that of married couples. Not only does the couple see little, if any, improvement to their savings, but they take on greater constraints without the necessary level of commitment and intentionality to withstand their burden.

Cohabitation helps test compatibility.

The growth of cohabitation is linked to two different views of marriage. The "low view" of marriage believes that love is all that matters and that marriage is nothing more than a legal document. This view of marriage became widespread among young people in the 1970s and 1980s, when cohabitation began rising in American culture. More recently, however, men and women justify cohabitation out of a "high view" of marriage. With the divorce rate hovering between 40 percent and 50 percent,

many adults have a strong desire to avoid divorce and succeed in marriage, and they believe that "trying on" marriage and testing their compatibility through cohabitation will help ensure future marital stability, happiness, and success.

Unfortunately, cohabitation is not a good test for compatibility. Even viewing relationships in this way habituates each partner to weighing obstacles and tensions on a type of "compatibility" scale—often against personal satisfaction. It habituates each partner to put his or her own comfort and preferences above those of the other, and to be critical of the other person's shortcomings. If the scale is tipped in the "incompatible" direction, there is always the option of failure and exit.

For those couples who do reach marriage, these habits often remain or reappear, and they prove destructive to a happy, stable marriage. In marriage, a man and woman enter into an indissoluble bond, characterized by mercy and fidelity. The only scale is that of virtue and truth. Their attitude must always be pro-relational, directed at finding a way forward together and not giving up on one another or the relationship. **No matter how committed a cohabiting couple may be, nobody would say that their commitment is indissoluble**.

We Go Together

Rate the statements below on the following scale,
circling the corresponding number:

1. As a couple, our compatibility is...	5	4	3	2	1
2. My love for my fiancé(e) is...	5	4	3	2	1
3. My faith and love for Jesus is...	5	4	3	2	1
4. My interest in marriage is...	5	4	3	2	1
5. My level of commitment to this relationship is...	5	4	3	2	1
6. My willingness to sacrifice is...	5	4	3	2	1

5 - Absolute
4 - Strong
3 - Moderate
2 - Weak
1 - None

Add up your responses. If your total is...

25–30 points — Why aren't you married already?

19–24 points — You're on your way! Use this time of preparation to grow in faith, trust, unity, and understanding.

13–18 points — Your road to marriage may be long and hard. Take some time to discern your true desires and bring your concerns honestly to your fiancé(e). Seek outside help before committing further.

6–12 points — Do you really want to be here? Strongly consider whether you truly belong with your partner or on the road to marriage.

You're not done yet! Share your responses and tally with your fiancé(e). If you're surprised by what you see, don't dismay. God has a plan for you both, and together you can find the truth.

Cohabitation ensures against future divorce.

Within the context of cohabitation, there are many factors and variations: whether a couple drifts into cohabitation or makes a clear decision to prepare for marriage, the respective age(s) of the partners, timing (that is, moving in before vs. after engagement), the number of times an individual has cohabited (that is, serial cohabitation), and other relationship constraints, such as a child. Couples who drift into living together, who move in before making a clear decision to marry, who are young, or who have cohabited with one or more people other than their spouse are at an increased risk for divorce. On the other hand, those who make a clear decision to marry before deciding to live together and who only cohabit with their spouse fare better in marriage on multiple measures.

This does not mean, however, that once a couple is engaged they should feel free to live together, or that living together is a good idea if there is mutual commitment. Engagements can be, and in some cases are, called off. Furthermore, some studies show that the risk of **divorce is associated with premarital sex itself**. One could therefore argue that cohabitation is risky for those hoping to avoid divorce simply on the basis of its connection to premarital sex and intimacy.

Transitioning to Marriage

The Church wants to help couples enter into marriage with as few risks as possible, overcome any challenges, and transition into sacramental marriage in the best way possible. If you are cohabiting and preparing for marriage, you are already on the right track. Although cohabitation is associated with greater risk in marriage, you can choose to continue on a risky path or begin practicing now the attitudes and behaviors that best prepare you for a healthy and happy marriage.

It is important that you make a sincere, deliberative decision to marry and do not drift into what seems to be the next natural phase. A happy marriage is not sustained by a one-time decision made the day you agree to marry. Marriage begins with a decision to commit to your spouse and is sustained by a daily decision to live out that commitment and to love each other unconditionally.

In marriage, we take on greater responsibility for the well-being of our spouse. Out of love, we make an effort to improve ourselves and accept the privilege of helping each other to seek, know, follow, and love Christ and his teachings. Most engaged couples already understand that they should act in each other's best interest. However, they may not realize that the spiritual and moral dimensions of our lives often affect the physical and emotional. If we understand how the Church's teachings are compatible with science and human reason and lead to human flourishing, the choice to live separately and chastely before marriage makes sense. **Chastity not only disposes a couple for less risk in marriage but also prepares their souls to receive marital grace** and to express their love with creativity, self-control, and selflessness.

It is easy for sexual intimacy to distract from and overshadow other ways of knowing and loving a person. When a couple lives separately and practices chastity, they have to find other ways to spend time together, gauge their compatibility, and express their affection. They share in each other's lives in a way fitting to any deep and sincere friendship—which is what marital love must be founded on.

The chaste lifestyle also creates more opportunities to look beyond the relationship and toward engaging family, friends, and colleagues together. These communities will prove a necessary source of support as you prepare for and enter married life. Mindful of confidentiality, **you will need the perspective of friends and family who know you and your loved one well** as you encounter difficult decisions and obstacles in your relationship.

In addition, allow your relationship to function and develop within a community of faith, welcoming God and his Church into your activities and decisions. Through the sacraments and your relationships with Jesus, you and your future spouse will find the sustenance and guidance to enter confidently into marriage and to live your marriage well.

Cohabitation offers little by way of actual marriage preparation. But the Church, with its wisdom and grace, offers much. If you have already taken a chance on cohabitation, the riskier road to marriage, why not now take a chance on the joy of lifelong, faithful love?

Your Story of Salvation

The Sexuality chapter describes marital chastity as a "story of salvation," which begins with "attraction and evolves over time into a deep love born of commitment." Describe your journey to marital chastity, beginning with first lessons and experiences and ending with a committed and holy sexuality with your spouse.

If you're currently cohabitating or in a sexual relationship, focus on your progress and describe steps and changes you can make to develop chastity in your lives. How will you overcome your challenges and lead each other to a lifetime of sacramental marriage?

For Reflection and Discussion

1. Share with one another your initial reasons for cohabiting. What were your intentions for the relationship and future intimacy when you made that decision? Do any of the three myths sound familiar or ring true for you?

2. Discuss how your views about cohabitation have changed since reading this chapter. How can chastity help you prepare for marriage? What would it mean to be chaste from now until after the wedding?

3. What are the pros and cons of living apart vs. together before marriage? If you disagree with living apart or being chaste, share your reasons for that position and discuss the real and potential effects and consequences of that decision.

4. Think about how you begin and end your days, how you prepare to leave your home and to go to sleep. What important activities do you need to accomplish each day? What can be left for later? List the five most important and the five least important parts of your daily routine.

A. *Most important*
-
-
-
-
-

B. *Least important*
-
-
-
-
-

5. How much time do you need to spend alone? What time of day do you enjoy being by yourself to get things done or just to relax? Discuss your needs and how these needs can best be met once you are married. Discuss whether you will need to plan any areas of your home for individual time or for any separate hobbies you have.

My Thoughts

_____
_____
_____
_____
_____
_____
_____
_____
_____
_____
_____
_____
_____
_____
_____
_____
_____
_____
_____
_____
_____

Annulment and Convalidation

Joann Heaney-Hunter, PhD

In this chapter...

- Christian marriage is called to be permanent.
- The essence of the annulment process is identical across the globe.
- Civil marriages are recognized by the Church through *convalidation*.

The *Catechism* asserts that the **marriage of two baptized persons is a sacrament, indissoluble and open to life**, and celebrated in the presence of the Church's minister and other witnesses in a church building (*CCC* 1631–1632). Despite this clear statement of practice, for many reasons a substantial number of couples do not follow the Church's teaching on the celebration of marriage.

Many Catholics, even active ones, may not fully understand the nuances of the Church's teachings on marriage. For example, pastors and other ministers report anecdotes of people who said they didn't marry in the Church because they were not confirmed or because their partner was not Catholic. These **Catholics were not turned away; they simply did not present themselves** because someone, usually a relative or friend, told them that they couldn't marry in the Church. These couples are quite surprised when they hear that their legal civil marriage can be affirmed in a Catholic ceremony known as convalidation.

There are also misunderstandings about how the Catholic Church regards divorce and second marriages. In fact, a 2011 study conducted by **CARA** (the Center for Applied Research in the Apostolate) showed that only 15 percent of active Catholics seek an annulment after a divorce. We can draw more than one conclusion from this statistic:

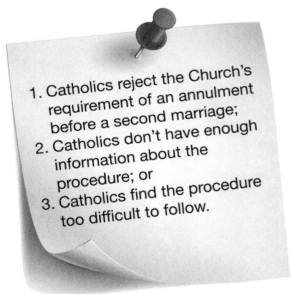

1. Catholics reject the Church's requirement of an annulment before a second marriage;
2. Catholics don't have enough information about the procedure; or
3. Catholics find the procedure too difficult to follow.

The Church, therefore, has an opportunity to provide pastoral care to these couples. This chapter guides couples seeking annulment or convalidation in the Church. It explains the respective processes and how they can bring healing and hope.

Unveiling the Truth

The following statements have been associated with the Church's teachings on marriage. Are they true or false? If they're false, can you reword the statements to make them true?

1. Catholics who divorced are guilty of sin.   T   F

2. The Church doesn't recognize civil marriages.   T   F

3. If you're not Catholic, you don't need an annulment.   T   F

4. Annulments are lengthy and expensive.   T   F

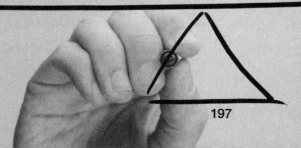

FACTS   MYTHS

Christian Marriage Throughout History

For centuries, there have been times when relationships fall apart, even when the couple has done everything possible to stay together. When spouses go through a divorce, the Church wants to do everything possible to care for them, up to and including the possibility of remarriage. The Church welcomes all who hope to reconnect with the faith community, and preparation for marriage after divorce and annulment is one way to begin a new journey.

From early in the Church's history, the marriage of Christians was presumed to be permanent. However, as early as the mid-first century, **when Paul's letters were written, there was recognition that some marriages should be dissolved**. In the case of two married pagans, if one person converted to Christianity and the other did not, conflicts could arise. This was especially true when Christian converts were subject to persecution or martyrdom. Therefore, if the pagan spouse did not wish to remain married to the Christian, the marriage was dissolved. In 1 Corinthians 7, Paul declares that these people are free to separate and marry again in peace (vs. 12–15). Except for that reason, the marriages of Christians were expected to be for life,

even if the parties were unhappy. Once the lifetime commitment was made, it was kept.

The Gospels also describe marriage practice among the followers of Jesus. Mark and Matthew note that divorce is not acceptable, citing Genesis 2, which declares that the two shall become one flesh (Mark 10:6–9; Matthew 19:3–6). Matthew notes that there may be an exception for *porneia*, a word the *New American Bible* translates as "unlawful" marriage and refers to incest; however, unlike the Jewish tradition, in which a husband was free to divorce his wife, **indissolubility was the norm for Christian marriage** (19:1-9; see also Matthew 5:31–32).

By the early fifth century, Latin-speaking theologians such as St. Augustine made the point that death is the only thing that ends marriage. Even if someone separated from a spouse for a serious reason such as adultery, that person would not be permitted to remarry until the death of the spouse. In the Greek-speaking church, the marriage bond existed even beyond the spouse's death. While a second marriage after the death of a spouse was tolerated, and divorce and remarriage were sometimes permitted after a period of penance, a person was considered virtuous if he or she remained unmarried. Saint John Chrysostom, writing in the early fifth century, encouraged a young widow to honor her first marriage so that she would be with her husband for all eternity in heaven.

A formal process of annulment, a declaration that the marriage never truly existed, began to emerge in the Church **by the beginning of the thirteenth century. This process evaluated whether or not the marriage was a true sacrament**. Ordinarily at that time, the only reason for an annulment was nonconsummation of the marriage. Even as the process evolved, it was not until the 1970s that annulments were granted for reasons other than severe mental illness, nonconsummation, or some other equally serious cause.

By the late 1970s, tribunals (church courts) in the United States began to acknowledge other causes for a declaration of nullity. For example, tribunal personnel evaluate the judgment and maturity of individuals and determine whether there might be psychological factors contributing to a person's inability to form a permanent relationship. Family-of-origin issues such as alcoholism or abuse, for example, could cloud a person's judgment and negatively influence the stability of a marriage.

The Annulment Process

The amount of time an annulment takes, the use of canonical advocates, and associated costs may vary from region to region, but the essence of the process—investigating the prior marriage through statements of the petitioner (the person filing for the annulment) and witnesses, and making a judgment as to whether or not the marriage was a true sacrament—is identical all over the world. Ordinarily, **the annulment process begins after the couple has concluded all divorce proceedings** and the petitioner presents the decree. The case may begin in his or her parish but will be adjudicated in a local diocesan tribunal.

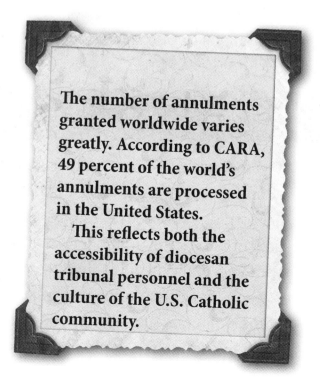

The number of annulments granted worldwide varies greatly. According to CARA, 49 percent of the world's annulments are processed in the United States.

This reflects both the accessibility of diocesan tribunal personnel and the culture of the U.S. Catholic community.

Intake and Information Gathering

The petitioner provides basic information about himself or herself and the former spouse. Required information, when applicable, includes:

- Names and addresses
- Dates of birth
- Names and religions of all sets of parents
- Dates and locations of baptism(s) and marriage
- Date of the divorce
- Number of children from the union
- Any previous or subsequent marriages, including information about a future spouse (if applicable)

Most tribunals require copies of the petitioner's baptismal certificate, Catholic marriage certificate, and divorce papers. In some dioceses, the process takes place by phone; in others, it is conducted in person by a canonical advocate. These personnel are specially trained and thoroughly understand the annulment process.

The petitioner then works with the intake official to develop a brief statement about why he or she believes that an annulment should be granted. The statement should **describe what was missing right from the start of the relationship**, not just the beginning of the marriage, because only a marriage where a key element is missing before the wedding can be annulled.

Petitioner's Essay and Statements

The petitioner writes an extensive essay about his or her life and that of his or her former spouse. The essay includes a description of the petitioner's and former spouse's early life, including the dynamics of each family, and a thorough exploration of the dating relationship. It continues with an evaluation of the wedding day (to see if there were any problems at the ceremony or reception) and an analysis of when the marital problems began. This can be a challenging task, and some people find it daunting and emotionally upsetting. While some say the essay dredges up elements of a painful past, it is necessary to provide information that will help tribunal officials determine whether or not an annulment can be granted.

The petitioner will also provide statements from witnesses who can corroborate the information presented in the essay. Ideally, the witnesses are people who have known the couple before and during the marriage and can speak to the challenges faced by the couple. Many dioceses even prefer that at least some of the witnesses be outside the petitioner's immediate family.

Hearing and Decision

An assigned judge evaluates the essays for completeness, and the petitioner is contacted to set up a hearing date. This hearing is not an adversarial process like a divorce trial. It simply makes sure that all the information is clear and allows the petitioner to answer questions that the judge might have. The judge presides over the hearing, and **a canon lawyer called the "defender of the bond" makes sure that all aspects of church procedure are followed correctly and that there are no inconsistencies** in the evidence.

Once a decision is reached, the case materials are sent to what is called the "court of second instance." This is a body of canon lawyers from a number of dioceses, who review its given region's annulment decisions. **Once they confirm the tribunal's declaration, the annulment is granted.**

Who Can Obtain an Annulment?

There are no hard-and-fast rules about who can obtain an annulment. Some annulled marriages were very short, and others spanned decades. The presence of children doesn't make a case more difficult, either. Individuals may have several children with their former spouse and still demonstrate that the marriage was not a true sacrament.

Some people are afraid that an annulment will render their children illegitimate. This is absolutely not the case. **When an annulment is granted, there was still a legal civil marriage.** The children of that union are legitimately the children of the legal marriage, and they won't be seen any differently after an annulment than they were after a divorce.

When Can I (Re)marry in the Church?

Of course, an annulment takes time to complete. Tribunals make it clear that the submission of paperwork is no guarantee that an annulment will ultimately be granted, so they warn against planning for a future wedding until the decree is final. In fact, **parishes are not permitted to save a date for a Church wedding until the process is concluded**, and couples may be required to participate in several sessions of post-annulment counseling before the decree is granted. Typically, a diocese will wait for a report from the therapist to release the decree.

The Catholic Church takes marriage seriously and wants to protect it from anything that would trivialize it. It also desires to help strengthen our connections with each other and with the Church itself. The teachings and regulations surrounding marriage and divorce exist to preserve the sacredness of the sacrament.

Be assured that parishes are ready and willing to help couples arrange their ceremonies as soon as the process is completed. While a couple waits, they can ask at the parish about what is needed to prepare for a marriage in the Church. Pastors and other pastoral staff members are happy to help and will do their best to accommodate their needs.

Convalidation

Many Catholic couples marry outside the Church. Some do so because one party is unable to marry in the Church as a result of a previous marriage. Many others prefer to hold their ceremony at a faraway destination, at the reception venue, or where it is more convenient for guests. In some countries, a civil marriage separate from the religious wedding ceremony is required for legal marriage rights. Couples may include prayers and Scripture readings in their civil ceremony and may even have a religious minister presiding at it, but **without the involvement of a Catholic parish, the wedding does not have the proper form** to be considered a Catholic marriage.

Some spouses later wish to develop stronger relationships with the Church community. Often, when parents come to the Church to baptize their first child, they are asked about their marriage for the baptismal record. Naturally, the Church cares for these children and desires to help the parents teach their children about their Catholic faith. **Parents who practice their faith regularly can teach their children by their own example of participating in sacraments** and praying with the faith community.

If a couple was unable to pursue a church wedding because of a previous divorce or related issue, a pastor or pastoral minister might find out the circumstances and assist them in beginning the annulment process. If possible, they will also offer the opportunity for convalidation, the blessing of an existing civil marriage, and provide the appropriate pastoral care so they can celebrate the sacraments.

How Does Convalidation Work?

All convalidations are governed by the rules of both Church and state. For example, in some states, a couple must file for a new marriage license before a convalidation can take place. The couple must follow the rules of the state before any Catholic marriage ceremony can take place.

Couples seeking convalidation usually follow a procedure similar to that of other couples preparing for a marriage in the Church. They complete a premarriage intake, which insures that they are free to marry in the Church. Some dioceses require the couples to complete a premarriage inventory, and there may be a period of "marriage preparation"—education and spiritual formation on Catholic teaching and marriage—just as with any first marriage. (*Done under the direction of a parish leader or minister, this workbook fulfills many marriage-preparation requirements*.) Once all these elements are completed, **the couple renews their vows at a Catholic ceremony**, with friends and family celebrating their new connection to the Church.

Some people ask what sort of ceremonies are "allowed" for convalidations. Customs vary, but it is safe to say that a convalidation ceremony looks very similar to any other wedding. They range from a simple celebration with immediate family and friends to an elaborate gala with many attendants and all the trimmings. Regardless of the ceremony's style, a convalidation is a time to rejoice, because couples have chosen to have their marriage blessed by the Church.

If I Knew Then...

People who remarry, reunite, or renew their marriage vows have the unique opportunity to view their relationship(s) from an external viewpoint. One major goal of marriage preparation is to facilitate the internal reflection and mutual dialogue necessary for personal and relational maturation.

Complete each statement below with a word or phrase that best expresses your beliefs or feelings.

1. When I think about my (previous) spouse, I...

_____

_____

2. My biggest regret to this point is...

_____

_____

3. When I met my current partner, I...

_____

_____

4. Going forward, the changes I would expect are...

_____

_____

For Reflection
and Discussion

1. Does the Church's history and position on divorce and remarriage change how you feel about the marriage you are preparing for now? Why or why not?

2. Discuss how your families of origin understand divorce and remarriage. What are the differences, if any? Have your notions on divorce changed since childhood? If so, how?

3. What step or part of the annulment or convalidation process seems most challenging? Why?

4. (a) What are the possible benefits to yourself and this marriage of having experienced the annulment process?

   (b) Discuss how convalidating your marriage will benefit yourrelationship and the intimacy therein. What changes do you expect, if any, in your religious practices and relationship with God?

My Thoughts

Interchurch and Interfaith Marriages

Daniel J. Olsen, PhD

In this chapter...

- The Catholic Church values mixed-religion marriages.
- Common challenges surround the wedding and children.
- Let your communities guide and support you.

in·ter·church mar·riage

/ˌin(t)ərˈ/CHərCH/ /ˈmerij/

A marriage between a baptized Catholic and another baptized Christian (Lutheran, Episcopal, Orthodox, Reformed, and more). These marriages have also been called "interdenominational," "ecumenical," or simply "mixed marriages," and presume a level of church involvement.

in·ter·faith mar·riage

/ˌin(t)ərˈfāTH/ /ˈmerij/

A marriage involving spouses from different religious traditions (nonbaptized, Jewish, Muslim, Hindu, and others). This may also include the marriage of a Christian to an atheist or a nonbeliever.

With few exceptions, religious traditions and communities agree that **marriage is an important social institution that forges religious, cultural, and family bonds.** The wedding ritual is a foundational event in the life of the couple, which publicly proclaims their various commitments to faith, family, and spouse. What happens, however, when one marries outside of one's religious tradition? How does one foster a lasting, loving union when one's religious practices and beliefs do not easily mesh with those of one's spouse-to-be? How does one balance diverse familial and cultural assumptions within a stable, unified home? Interchurch and interfaith couples often face unique challenges, but these marriages can also bring unique opportunities and gifts to their families and faith communities.

In the United States today, **Roman Catholics marry members from other Christian churches or religious communities more than 40 percent of the time.**

Defining Your Faith

To make your faiths clearer, complete the sentences below.

- In terms of religion, I identify myself as...

_____

_____

- I believe God is...

_____

_____

- The religious text(s) or creed(s) I follow are...

_____

_____

- I would describe my spirituality as...

_____

_____

- When faced with social or moral difficulties, I...

_____

_____

- When I think of death or an afterlife, I...

_____

_____

Depending on your religious upbringing and beliefs, you may use words that your fiancé(e) may or may not understand. How would you define or describe the following terms?

- Covenant:

- Faith:

- Grace:

- Justice:

- Law:

- Sacrament:

Interchurch Marriage: A Gift and a Sacrament

Since both parties are Christians and united in a commonly recognized baptism, interchurch marriages have a distinctive giftedness. As recent popes have observed, **interchurch families can contribute a great deal toward the goal of full Christian unity.** Living their lives together while bonded to diverse Christian traditions, interchurch couples can more readily identify the challenges that remain on the ecumenical road, even as they celebrate the gifts that Christians share in the present. Interchurch couples can help their friends, families, and churches move past current and common misunderstandings and fears.

Further signaling their giftedness, the Catholic Church identifies interchurch marriages as a "sacrament," just as it does with marriages between two Catholics. As a sacrament, Christian marriage offers couples the grace to model the love that Christ shows for the church (Ephesians 5:21–33). Other Christian churches might not recognize marriage as a sacrament, but they clearly agree that marriage is a holy covenant uniting the couple to God and one another through love.

212

Dialogue and Relationships

Various religious leaders have placed great value in coming to learn more about the beliefs and practices that members from other religions hold dear. This dialogue often begins with establishing a personal and prayerful relationship with practitioners of other faiths. Establishing a friendship allows one to enter into a meaningful discussion about religious values, beliefs, and practices. **Interreligious relationships that lead to marriage, then, can uniquely model interreligious dialogue** by placing their discussions about values within a context centered in love and respect. As these spouses come to grow in their love for each other, their respect for their partner's religious convictions will often grow, too. This understanding and love can be a powerful gift in an increasingly pluralistic world.

For Christians, **God is Trinity, three-in-one, the very model of relational love** that all humans seek. Christian spouses are called to mirror this love as best they can, striving for friendship and unity in the midst of their challenges. In order to be faithful to your vows and promises, you will have to be intentional about your religious choices and practices. Allow this intentionality to become a life-giving spring to nourish your holy union.

Challenges to Interchurch Marriage

The Wedding

As you prepare for your wedding, **each spouse will likely feel duties and obligations to their own churches**. It is important to begin to negotiate these feelings as a couple in light of your love for one another. Coming to a consensus about how best to move forward with the wedding will be an important first step in forging a lasting union.

Start a conversation with both of your local pastoral leaders (pastor, minister, priest, or deacon). Within these conversations, key questions will emerge about where and how you plan to celebrate your marriage. **For Catholics who wish to be married in an interchurch marriage, permission must be given from the local bishop.** To receive this permission, Catholics are required to promise to remain faithful to the Catholic Church, promise to do "all in their power" to raise their children in the Catholic Church (more on this later), and commit to understanding what the Church teaches about marriage.

These promises, as well as seeking permission for an interchurch marriage, are meant to ensure that the marriage is freely and consciously entered into, while giving the Catholic party the support and guidance they need from his/her church. Likewise, other Christian communities often uphold a sense of obligation in these matters, although they may have different procedures and means of expressing it.

If the decision is made to have the wedding in a Catholic parish, it will be important to consider whether it is desirable to have the wedding service without Eucharist (holy Communion) or within a full Catholic Mass. **Most Catholic pastors will suggest that the couple not include the Eucharist at an interchurch wedding** since it can invite hurt or confusion due to current restrictions on eucharistic hospitality. This is particularly the case if many non-Catholics are expected to be in attendance.

If it is decided to have the wedding in a location other than a Catholic parish, the Catholic party needs to receive permission from the bishop or his designate. Also, only one priest/minister can officially preside at the wedding. But it is always a wonderful sign of support and unity if a priest/minister is present from both churches. Saying a prayer or offering a blessing for the couple can do much to signal support and acceptance of the union from both churches.

Family and Formation of Children

Your choice to marry a Christian from another church may invite negative responses from your extended family or in-laws. While challenging, these interactions can give you a unique opportunity to **share the love that you have for your spouse and Christ with others, and to learn more about yourself, your partner's family**, and the diverse tapestry that exists within the Christian community. These discussions may be tinged with fear, misunderstanding, or even dislike, but they can result in growth if handled with patience and honesty.

Other challenges may occur with the birth of your first child. It is essential to begin the conversation about how you will integrate your children into the fabric of your marriage before your wedding. As noted earlier, the Catholic spouse is required "to make a sincere promise to do all in his or her power so that all children are baptized and brought up in the Catholic Church" (*Canon* 1125). This promise reminds both spouses of the Catholic community's interest in nurturing the child's faith. Catholic bishops and priests also make a commitment to you at this time to help you foster unity as a couple and to aid you in educating your children religiously. They are "to take care that the Catholic spouse and the children born of a mixed marriage do not lack the spiritual help to fulfill their obligations and are to help spouses foster the unity of conjugal and family life" (*Canon* 1128). Use their commitment, and the commitment of all Christian ministers, to solidify your union and raise your children as faithful Christians.

The Bible calls all Christians to unity.

1 SAMUEL 20:42

"The two of us have sworn by the name of the LORD: 'The LORD shall be between you and me, and between your offspring and mine forever.'"

Name three ways you have reached out to your future spouse's church, faith, family, or culture.

1. _____
2. _____
3. _____

ACTS 14:27

"They called the church together and reported what God had done with them…"

Name three ways you intend to bring your spouse and your marriage into your church, faith, family, or culture

1. _____
2. _____
3. _____

1 CORINTHIANS 1:10

"I urge you…that all of you agree in what you say, and that there be no divisions among you, but that you be united in the same mind and in the same purpose."

Name three religious principles or practices that you both cherish.

1. _____
2. _____
3. _____

PHILIPPIANS 2:13

"For God is the one who, for his good purpose, works in you both…"

Name three ways you see God working in or through your fiancé(e), or three ways in which he or she exemplifies righteousness or holiness.

1. _____
2. _____
3. _____

Challenges to Interfaith Marriage

Interfaith marriage brings with it unique and often difficult challenges that should be addressed openly and honestly. While some religious groups do not permit interfaith marriages, Catholics do. Unions between a Catholic and a non-baptized spouse are called marriage with a "disparity of cult." **Though not considered a sacrament, it is a valid marriage if the Catholic spouse receives proper permission from the local bishop** (*Canon* 1125). To receive this "dispensation" to marry, **Catholics are required to declare that they will remain faithful to the Catholic Church and promise to do "all in their power" to raise their children as Catholics**.

They also commit to coming to a clear understanding about what their Church teaches about marriage. These promises are meant to ensure that the interfaith marriage bond is freely and validly entered into, while helping the Catholic party live out their life in Christ through the Church.

The Wedding

Because many other religious communities also uphold a strong sense of obligation in these matters, **the best way forward is to discuss your wedding plans with your local religious leaders**. Coming to a consensus about where and how to celebrate your unity will become an important foundational piece for your life together. If the wedding is held in a Catholic parish, a service tailored to your situation will be used. Again, if the wedding will not be held in a Catholic parish, the Catholic party must seek permission from the bishop to hold it elsewhere. While only one minister can preside at the wedding, **consider how a minister or leader from both faiths could take part as a show of support**.

Also keep in mind that the wedding includes much more than just a service in a sacred space. Song, dance, ritual, and food often accompany these culturally significant moments. Each spouse and his or her family will likely hold assumptions about where and how the wedding and related events will unfold. It is important to **balance these expectations in light of the similarities that you share as a couple**. Discerning similarity and balancing your differing viewpoints will become a key part of your life together. Beginning that exploration and negotiation now will help you establish a lasting interfaith union.

Family and Formation of Children

Your choice to marry a person from another religion may invite cautionary, or even critical, responses from those who love you most. Although difficult, these interactions can provide you with an opportunity to share the love you have for your spouse while learning more about your faith as you listen to spousal concerns. They undoubtedly want the best for you, and balancing their thoughts with your own calls for patience. Even when a complete agreement cannot be achieved, **your willingness to enter into dialogue about religious and cultural issues raises awareness about the values and convictions shared among many people and traditions**. This is a gift for all involved and for the world.

The birth of your first child will likely create challenges. This may not be an immediate concern, but *you should begin to discuss how you could integrate a child into your family* (see *Canon* 1125). **The Catholic spouse's promise reminds both spouses of the necessity and value of the sacraments, especially baptism, held by the Christian faith**.

The non-Catholic spouse may also have similar religious expectations or obligations. There is often no easy solution to these matters, but **if a consensus on how to raise the child religiously can be arrived at early on, the marriage and family life to follow will benefit**. Remain in dialogue with your local religious leaders, discerning with them the best way forward as a couple. If they express reservations about your relationship, try to see it as concern for your well-being and an expression of their deep religious convictions. Do your best to listen to them and explore the questions of religious identity and family unity that they are raising.

Cultural Differences and Understandings of Marriage

Often when members of two different faiths are represented in a marriage, cultural differences also become apparent. Marriage and its purpose may be defined somewhat differently by your respective religions or cultures. Furthermore, many Americans believe the core purpose of marriage to be the ultimate expression and fostering of a loving companionship. In this perspective, one seeks, finds, and then commits to one's "soul mate." To this praiseworthy sense of companionate love, though, most religions and many cultures would add a strong commitment to extended family, religious beliefs and practices, and faith formation of children. **Loving someone is not always viewed as the only requirement (or even the most important requirement) for entering into a lifelong bond.**

It is important to be aware of these differences and to seek the truth together. Thinking through how you define marriage and its primary goals, while comparing that vision with what your extended families, cultures, and religions offer is an important step in preparing for marriage—perhaps the most important step. Take the time to explore these elements and issues. **Share your feelings with each other openly and honestly, and remain attentive to your similarities, especially in terms of core values.** Those values attracted you to one another in the first place.

Perspectives on Marriage and Family

Answer the following questions, then share your responses with each other.

1. Prior to marriage, I strongly desire that my partner: (Check all that apply.)

   ☐ Attend a religious service within my community.
   ☐ Convert to my religion/faith.
   ☐ Receive approval from my parents/family.
   ☐ Host or attend an engagement party or wedding shower.
   ☐ Make specific promises (please specify): _____

2. After marriage, I strongly desire that my spouse: (Check all that apply.)

   ☐ Attend religious services with me occasionally.
   ☐ Attend religious services with me regularly (or exclusively).
   ☐ Allow me to attend religious services within my community regularly (or exclusively).
   ☐ Raise our children within his/her faith community.
   ☐ Allow me to raise our children within my faith community.
   ☐ Join me in raising our children together in faith.

3. I strongly desire the following traditions on our wedding day:
   (Check and describe all that apply.)

   ☐ Garments/Wardrobe: _____
   ☐ Texts/Readings: _____
   ☐ Music: _____
   ☐ Dance: _____
   ☐ Food/Drink (consider Communion and the use of alcoholic beverages):
   _____
   ☐ Candles: _____
   ☐ Ministers/People: _____
   ☐ Other: _____

4. I strongly object to the following traditions on our wedding day:
   (Check and describe all that apply.)

   ☐ Garments/Wardrobe: _____
   ☐ Texts/Readings: _____
   ☐ Music: _____
   ☐ Dance: _____
   ☐ Food/Drink (consider Communion and the use of alcoholic beverages):
   _____
   ☐ Candles: _____
   ☐ Ministers/People: _____
   ☐ Other: _____

Did any of the responses surprise you? Why or why not?

For Reflection and Discussion

Interchurch Marriage

1. Discuss the common beliefs and practices you share as Christians, then identify the diverse beliefs and practices of your churches and/or denominations. Identify ways you can live these out as a couple (including worship, holidays, home prayer, and financial contributions to your churches).

2. Where and how will you celebrate your wedding? What processes and procedures must you attend to so that your marriage is properly recognized and supported by your churches? Can you involve both pastoral leaders in your wedding and marriage? If so, how?

3. How have your families reacted to your choice to marry a Christian from a different church? How have you invited them to be a part of your wedding and lifelong marriage?

4. How do you plan to educate your children in the Christian faith? Where will they be baptized, and how will they be raised as Christians in light of your respective values, beliefs and practices?

5. To whom (or where) do you plan on turning for answers, advice, and continued Christian formation? When questions about Christian practices and beliefs arise, do you involve your priests, pastors, ministers, and fellow Christians in the conversation?

Interfaith Marriage

1. Discuss the similarities you have found in your religious traditions and then consider the differences you have noticed in your beliefs and practices. What is the purpose of marriage according to your religion and/or culture?

2. Discuss how you each intend to live out your respective beliefs and practices as a wedded couple, including religious practices, holiday celebrations, prayer in the home, financial attitudes and expectations, and raising of children.

3. Discuss how your families have reacted to your choice to marry someone from a different religion.

4. Reflect on the ways you might invite family members to be a part of your wedding ceremony or celebration. Discuss these possibilities and how this could help them become a part of your marriage.

5. Review and discuss the processes and procedures you need to attend to so that your marriage is recognized and supported by your religious communities. Do you have a plan to involve both pastoral leaders in your wedding and marriage? If so, how?

_____
_____
_____
_____
_____
_____
_____
_____
_____
_____
_____
_____
_____
_____
_____
_____
_____
_____
_____
_____
_____
_____

Military Marriage

Fr. John Paul Echert

In this chapter...

- Living the military life as a couple
- Dealing with separation, relocation, and injury
- Using the resources and support available to you

Military service is a shared sacrifice and a way of life. This is particularly the case for active-duty couples but true for Guard and Reserve couples as well. Since military service is much more than a job, it is vitally important that you both are committed to its unique demands upon marriage and family. If either of you have concerns or reservations, now is the time to carefully discuss these and work out agreeable resolutions. Remember: Even though military service is not necessarily lifelong like marriage, military members are obliged by their oaths to fulfill the terms of service to which they have committed.

If you are an active-duty couple, chances are that you are working with a military Catholic chaplain and that your marriage preparation is guided by the norms of the Archdiocese for the Military Services. If you are a Guard or Reserve couple, a Catholic chaplain may be available to you if you are not working with a civilian priest. Whichever the case, be sure to **contact the chaplain or pastor months in advance** of your wedding to arrange for your preparation and wedding details. This is especially important if there are special considerations that may bear upon your preparation, the wedding, or the marriage itself.

After the military member presents the marriage license to the personnel office, you newlyweds are legally and formally a military couple. You will find a widely extended family in the armed forces, but at the local levels military life in many ways resembles a biological family. You share common missions and commitments, many facilities and activities, and you have common interests and values. You also have a special community and bond that can be a great source of support.

Meet the Challenges Together

Two top priorities essential to successful marriages are Christ and communication—the two C's. If you keep Christ at the center of your marriage and you communicate well as a couple, you are on the common path to success. Other priorities such as family, friends and military career, will naturally fall into place. Many military bases offer retreats and programs for strengthening marriages that focus upon setting priorities and strengthening communication skills. Once married, ask your chaplain about such opportunities.

Chain of Command

1. Rank the following in order of priority to yourself and your life.

2. Enter your fiancé(e)'s responses in the appropriate column.

3. Finally, together build a shared list of priorities that create a framework for your values and future decisions.

Priority	His Rank	Her Rank	Our Rank
Commitment/Loyalty			
Communication			
Community (base, town, friends)			
God/Christ			
Family/Children			
Fidelity (trust, honesty)			
Love (intimacy, mercy)			
Military/Career (company, division, chief)			
President of the United States			
Spouse			

Separation

During their engagement, many couples already deal with difficulties that arise from physical separation. In the military, **separation can be a matter of days, weeks, or much longer.** During the Iraq War some soldiers were deployed for nearly two years, but now, in large part due to the stress that this placed upon families, one year of separation is the upper limit.

You have probably heard the saying, "Absence makes the heart grow fonder." This is not always the case, though **in strong, healthy relationships, couples can find new ways of keeping close during a physical separation.** Decades ago, some remote assignments meant lengthy periods of isolation, the only contact with loved ones coming in monthly mail drops.

Today, technology makes frequent, even daily, contact with spouses much easier, if the mission allows it. Couples and families connect through morale calls, texts, emails, social media, and even "snail mail." Ironically, some couples end up communicating more frequently and more intimately while physically separated

than when face-to-face. But a caution is in order. **Couples need to be especially sensitive to the impact their words can have upon each other**, for good or bad. Nothing is worse than a morale call or email exchange that ends poorly, regardless of good intentions. In advance of separation, couples who have some common agreement and understanding as to what sorts of things to share can avoid such negative circumstances. Some couples want to know everything from a distance; others do not. Know yourself and your partner.

Ever hear the expression, "There are no atheists in foxholes?" Sadly, some people do not believe in God, but for many others, religion becomes particularly important during times of separation and stress. Many a troop on deployment finds God for the first time or rediscovers religion. Christian marriage is a covenant in Christ, and so the shared faith of the couple can transcend the miles. **For those couples who are actively practicing their faith, by all means keep it up, at home and deployed**. For those who have drifted away for one reason or another, take this time to rediscover your faith, which will sustain you in your life's challenges.

Reintegration

Of course, after separation comes reunion. Usually, the longer the separation, the more exciting the reunion. We have all seen images of troops returning home from lengthy deployments, straight into the loving embrace of spouses and families.

But just as separation requires some adjustments, so does reconstitution. Often the spouse who remained home has assumed responsibilities that are normally shared. Letting go of these can sometimes involve a tug of war. If there are children, then the spouse at home has had the additional challenge of being a temporary single parent.

Be patient and understanding with each other as well as with your children, who may also require extra time and attention to readjust. Sometimes shifting from the regimented life of deployment to family and civilian life is a struggle and may simply take time.

The good news is that the military has some wonderful programs, people, and resources to assist members, couples, and families. This assistance typically begins prior to the actual deployment, continues during the separation, and follows up in the days and weeks after returning home. For that matter, **when issues related to a deployment remain unresolved or later arise, help continues for as long as it is needed**.

One of the primary programs is the Yellow Ribbon Reintegration Program. Some of you may have already participated in one of these. One of the many features of these deployment/reintegration programs is that they bring together couples who have never experienced military separation with those who have. Seasoned deployers will tell you that each time they deployed, the more lessons they learned, including those related to marriage and family.

Couples can interact and share insights and experiences. Again, what works for one couple may not work for another, but most couples who are new to military life are eager to hear from others.

Relocation

Many grow up in the security of stability: a familiar neighborhood, one parish, and schools in which we make close friends. Military life is typically not so stable. In addition to times of separation, permanent changes of station (PCS) are a common feature. Some military careers and branches

You Are Not Alone

Military programs provide a support system that can be spiritual, emotional, and sometimes physical. For instance, while one airman was deployed, his home was damaged by a flood. Fellow airmen back home went to his house, on their own dime and time, and repaired much of the damage. Bravo!

of service entail more changes and relocations than others, but **an entire active-duty career in one location is quite rare**. As with any major transition, including from the single to married life, it is important to keep in mind that transitions are only temporary. Most of us do not like upheaval, but if you anticipate it and approach change with confidence as a couple, your marriage will likely become stronger.

The military has many resources to help with PCS (permanent change of station). Some are not available until you are legally married, but you should receive them shortly after. They include help in locating housing; financial benefits, including allowances for food and housing; and access to on-base facilities such as military department and grocery stores and recreational facilities and services. Depending upon size, location, and mission, many bases— both stateside and overseas—replicate a civilian community within their own secure gates. If or when you anticipate a PCS, be sure to do some prep and recon early on to insure a smooth transition.

Once you arrive at your new location, **do not isolate yourselves from your new communities** or withdraw from opportunities. Initial isolation in new circumstances can be a common tendency but generally is not helpful. When you get to a new location, a good place to start looking for ways to connect with others and find social activities is a base chapel or civilian parish. Also look for the family service centers and representatives that can provide you with information about the base, local community, and upcoming social and recreational activities. Take a risk and just start somewhere, then let your lives bloom wherever you are planted!

My Military Life

While aspects of military life may seem (or simply be) out of your control, there are ways to make the best out of even difficult situations. State your ideals by answering the questions below, then share your responses with each other.

1. I envision our military life lasting...
   - ☐ Fewer than 5 years
   - ☐ 6–12 years
   - ☐ 13–20 years
   - ☐ 21–40 years
   - ☐ A lifetime

2. In general, I see ourselves having...
   - ☐ A small group of close friends
   - ☐ Friends and family scattered across the country and globe
   - ☐ Friends and resources centered on our location
   - ☐ A large support network and active social life

3. If and when I am separated from my spouse, I'd prefer... (Check all that apply.)
   - ☐ Daily communications
   - ☐ Weekly communications
   - ☐ Monthly communications
   - ☐ Detailed communications
   - ☐ Communications surrounding our military life
   - ☐ Communications about the home/family
   - ☐ Communications to strengthen our intimacy
   - ☐ Only necessary facts

4. If we were relocated to another region of the United States, I'd prefer...
   - ☐ The Northeast
   - ☐ The Midwest
   - ☐ The South
   - ☐ The Pacific Northwest
   - ☐ The Southwest (California, Arizona)

5. If we were relocated overseas, I'd prefer... (no more than two)
   - ☐ Central America
   - ☐ South America
   - ☐ Western Europe
   - ☐ Eastern Europe / Russia
   - ☐ Africa
   - ☐ Southeast Asia
   - ☐ East Asia (China, Japan)
   - ☐ Australia / Pacific Islands
   - ☐ Arctic / Antarctic

6. My greatest fear about military life is...
   - ☐ Instability, especially within the marriage and family
   - ☐ Injury or disability
   - ☐ Mental/Social trauma
   - ☐ Death or widow(er)hood
   - ☐ Attack or combat
   - ☐ Moral or religious harm
   - ☐ Other: _____

Injury or Trauma

As much as we wish it were not so, the military has as its business the dangerous mission of going to war, and inevitably some members will return home with injuries, some quite serious. **For those who have experienced dangerous deployments, severe hardships, injury, or trauma, reintegration often presents more challenges** and requires patience.

For troops who have been in combat or on general alert, they may come home with a "locked and loaded" perspective still operative or lurking beneath the surface. Ordinary activities such as driving in rush-hour traffic may cause flashback images of driving in dangerous military convoys. Healthy readjustment to "normal life" typically happens within days and weeks, but if it stretches out longer and there are signs of unhealthy habits such as difficulties with sleep, depression, or excessive consumption of alcohol, **be sure to seek professional help**. While the bodies and minds of some military members have suffered much, their spirits can remain strong.

Wounded Warriors

The Soldier's and Airman's Creeds promise to never leave a fallen soldier or airman behind. If you ever face this hard reality, be strong for each other and work through it together. Remember your marriage vows— "in sickness and in health." Military chaplains are painfully aware of the risks that members accept and the occasional cost of their commitment. We pray that the ultimate sacrifice is not required of us, but it is a risk that military couples accept.

For stories and tips on overcoming these obstacles, visit the Wounded Warrior Project website.

Marital Infidelity and Divorce

In making a choice for someone in marriage you also choose against any other inappropriate action or relationship. This means that you don't let your eyes or imagination wander. **Even within a military setting, temptations run high**, so retain custody of your body, faculties, and self—starting today.

While most couples do not enter marriage intending divorce, unfortunately it is a far-too-common reality. In fact, certain features of military life such as separation can leave couples more vulnerable to bad decisions. However, you are not a statistic; the lifelong success of your marriage is within your control as a couple. **While a shaky marriage can be one of the worst stressors for a military couple, a solid marriage is one of their greatest reinforcements**. Begin with good habits and good faith, and if you ever find yourself in trouble, agree now to reach out for readily available help.

Look Ahead

Engaged couples may not think of preparing for retirement, but your vows are until death, so some thought at the start of marriage is appropriate, especially for military couples. Unlike civilian employment, which may change frequently, **military couples tend to make more long-term decisions related to careers**. The more years invested in military service, the more incentive to finish out a career to qualify for retirement benefits. Presently, military members qualify for retirement after a minimum of twenty years of service. Whatever you choose to do, **make sure you are of like mind and committed to your decision as a couple**.

The decision to join the military will be one of the biggest commitments of your lives, but commitment to marriage is even bigger. It is not simply a tour of duty. **Couples rightly want nothing less than the security and permanency Christian marriage offers**. You may be working already with a chaplain in your marriage preparation. If not, you will have many interactions with chaplains as a couple.

Believe it or not, precisely **because you are in the military, you have an incredible treasure chest of help**. Assemble a list of important resources and people. Many bases typically provide religious services for their members and families, including the Mass and sacraments. Explore your local communities, churches, and the member's chain of command. Get connected by volunteering or reaching out for help.

It almost goes without saying, but your family and friends are an indispensable source of strength and support, especially in stressful situations. Remember the campfire song: "Make new friends, but keep the old…" You will be making new friends constantly as you move through the military world, and you will continue to have family and friends back home as well.

Additional Military Resources

The following are types of services and organizations you are likely to encounter:

- Family service centers
- Family life consultants
- Veterans assistance programs
- Veteran service organizations
- Civilian community organizations
- Military OneSource
- Beyond the Yellow Ribbon
- Wounded Warrior Project

As you build your military marriage, create a united front.

MATTHEW 8:9 / LUKE 7:8

"I too am a person subject to authority, with soldiers subject to me."

Name two nonmilitary authorities you are subject to, and any person or thing for which you have authority.

1. _____

2. _____

3. _____

2 TIMOTHY 2:3

"Bear your share of hardship along with me like a good soldier of Christ Jesus."

Name three hardships you will face together as military spouses.

1. _____

2. _____

3. _____

NUMBERS 31:49

"Your servants have counted the soldiers under our command, and not one of us is missing."

Name three ways you can support your spouse and family in tough times.

1. _____

2. _____

3. _____

PSALM 27:1, 3

"The LORD is my light and my salvation; whom should I fear? ...Though an army encamp against me, my heart does not fear; Though war be waged against me, even then do I trust."

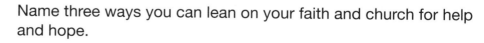

Name three ways you can lean on your faith and church for help and hope.

1. _____

2. _____

3. _____

For Reflection and Discussion

1. If only one of you is currently a military member, discuss what you both need in order to feel connected and supported.

2. Discuss your expectations related to your military career. If you are not in full agreement, talk about what you can do to work through unresolved issues.

3. Reflect on your experiences of being separated from one another. Share your feelings and discuss the best available means to communicate during future periods of separation.

4. Reflect on your hopes, fears, and expectations for future deployments and relocations. Share your plans for finding activities and resources within the military and civilian communities that interest and fulfill you as individuals and as a couple. *Agree on at least one that you both can be involved with now* to help ease your transition to married life.

5. Reflect on the friendships you have with other military individuals and couples. Discuss what opportunities you see now or shortly after your marriage to become connected with other military couples.

My Thoughts

239

About the Contributors (alphabetically)

Charles E. Bouchard, OP
Fr. Bouchard lives in Chicago, where he is Provincial of the Central Dominican Province. He is former professor and president of Aquinas Institute of Theology in St. Louis and continues to write and lecture on health-care ethics, spirituality, and morality. His most recent book from Liguori Publications is *Sexuality and Morality*.

Bridget Brennan
Bridget Brennan, a native of St. Louis, is the founder and president of the Cana Institute, which provides training, counseling, and support for married couples and families. She offers relationship coaching and teaches courses on marriage preparation to program leaders. She and her husband present retreats and workshops for engaged and married couples and coauthored *Claiming Our Deepest Desires: The Power of an Intimate Marriage* (Liturgical Press). A former director of religious education, Bridget holds degrees in religious studies and human relations.

Deacon Harold Burke-Sivers
Deacon Burke-Sivers founded and is president of Servant Enterprises, Inc., a Catholic evangelization and apologetics organization that coordinates speaking tours and seminars, retreats, and develops products and services that support marriage and family life. Deacon Harold lives in Portland, Oregon, with his wife, Colleen, and their four children.

Fr. John Paul Echert
Fr. Echert is a priest of the Archdiocese of St. Paul-Minneapolis and a senior Air Force chaplain for the 133rd Airlift Wing of the Minnesota Air National Guard. His service to civilian parishes and the military spans decades. He is also a former professor of sacred Scripture for the Saint Paul Seminary School of Divinity and adjunct faculty member at the University of St. Thomas in St. Paul. A Scripture forum expert for EWTN, he holds a licentiate in sacred Scripture from the Pontifical Biblical Institute in Rome.

David W. Fagerberg, PhD
Dr. Fagerberg teaches liturgical theology at the University of Notre Dame and is a former director and advisor to the Notre Dame Center for Liturgy. He is an accomplished author and holds multiple degrees, including a doctorate from Yale University. He and his wife, Elizabeth, have been married for more than forty years and have two adult sons.

Joann Heaney-Hunter, PhD
Dr. Heaney-Hunter teaches pastoral theology at St. John's University in New York. She holds a doctorate in theology from Fordham University and a master's in mental health counseling from Long Island University, both in New York state, where she is licensed to practice mental health counseling. She is an internationally recognized speaker, author, and educator on marriage and family ministry in the Catholic Church. She coauthored *Unitas*, a pair of couples and leaders guides on marriage preparation, for Crossroad Publishing.

Cassandra Hough
Cassandra Hough is the founder and senior advisor of the Love and Fidelity Network, a national program that equips the next generation of leaders with the arguments and resources they need to advocate for marriage, family, and sexual integrity. Previously known to some as Cassy DeBenedetto, she is an active voice against the college hookup culture in and around the Princeton community. Now married and the mother of three, she has been featured in *The New York Times*, *The Washington Post*, and elsewhere.

Karen Jiménez Robles, MD
Dr. Jiménez, born in Veracruz, Mexico, graduated medical school with an interest in natural family planning and earned her master's in human reproduction in 2007. In 2011, she studied, provided, and practiced the Creighton Method and NaPro Technology under Dr. Thomas Hilgers of the Pope Paul VI Institute for the Study of Human Reproduction in Omaha. In 2013, she opened the first such clinic in Latin America, offering couples training, support, diagnoses, and treatments that don't compromise Catholic faith or morals.

Phil Lenahan
In 1983, Phil Lenahan accepted an accounting position with Arthur Andersen and Co. After several years with the firm, he left to pursue a more balanced life. He spent eight years with the manufacturer Fleetwood Enterprises, then in 1995 accepted a CFO position at Catholic Answers. In 2005, Phil began working with Our Sunday Visitor to develop his popular program *7 Steps to Becoming Financially Free* and founded Veritas Financial Ministries, which equips people to manage their personal finances according to Catholic principles. He is married and the father of seven.

Coleen Kelly Mast
Coleen Kelly Mast, an internationally known author and speaker on Catholic family life, has assisted the United States Conference of Catholic Bishops and the Vatican on developing teachings on the family and human sexuality. She hosts the radio show *Mast Appeal* and cohosts *The Dr. Is In* on Ave Maria and EWTN Radio. She authored the Love and Life and Sex Respect chastity-education programs, and she gives Pre-Cana presentations. Coleen holds an honorary doctorate and a master's degree in health education. She is married and the mother of five.

Deborah Meister
Deborah Meister of St. Louis holds master's degrees in literature and theology, a graduate certificate in pastoral care, and certification in pastoral ministry (Archdiocese of St. Louis). She was an editor with Liguori Publications, and was the coordinator of family life with the Archdiocese of St. Louis, where she helped develop a comprehensive marriage-preparation program. With years of experience as an educator and parish minister, Meister helps parishes and publishers provide catechetical resources. She is married and the mother of two adult daughters.

Daniel J. Olsen, PhD
Dr. Olsen is assistant director of the Office for Ecumenical and Interreligious Affairs for the Archdiocese of Chicago and an adjunct professor of theology at St. Xavier University, Chicago, and The College of St. Scholastica in Duluth, Minnesota. He holds a doctorate in constructive theology from Loyola University Chicago. His dissertation explored the pastoral gifts and challenges to be found in the experiences of interchurch families. He lives in suburban Chicago with his wife and two young children.

David A. Smith, PhD
Dr. Smith is a professor in the Psychology Department at the University of Notre Dame, where he teaches and supervises doctoral marital therapy trainees. He is a licensed and board-certified psychologist and received his doctorate from SUNY Stony Brook. As director of the Marital Therapy and Research Clinic, he studies the links between depression and marital discord with observational studies of interspousal criticism and destructive marital attributions, at times using an experimental gaming model of forgiveness.